■SCHOLAST

Writing Lessons
for the Overhead

Responding to Literature

by Lola M. Schaefer

New York • Toronto • London • Auckland • Sydney
Mexico City • New Delhi • Hong Kong • Buenos Aires

Teaching *Resources*

Dedication

For the teachers who blend reading and writing
seamlessly each and every day

Acknowledgments

Thank you to Black's Mill Elementary School for the collaboration.

BRAVO! to editors Sarah Longhi and Joanna Davis Swing
who work diligently to produce the best instructional materials for teachers.
You're great, ladies!

Cover design by Jason Robinson
Interior design by Sarah Morrow

ISBN-13: 978-0-545-05403-4
ISBN-10: 0-545-05403-6

2 3 4 5 6 7 8 9 10   40   15 14 13 12 11 10 09

Contents

Introduction

Purpose for Writing Literature Responses

We ask students to write literature responses for several reasons: We want students to think more critically about what they read; it's one way to teach them story elements; literature responses are listed in the language arts standards; and responses blend reading and writing. But a sixth-grade student I know said it best: "We write literature responses to learn the best about ourselves." How profound.

When children think critically about the literature they read, they often see themselves in the resourceful, determined protagonists in the stories, people such as Marian Anderson (*When Marian Sang* by Pam Muñoz Ryan) or Brian Robeson (*Hatchet* by Gary Paulsen). They learn the impact that war, a natural disaster, or even an energy crisis can have on their lives from reading stories with strong settings like *Across the Blue Pacific* by Louise Borden. They see how they can meet challenges, and they view their role in the world community with a new sense of importance after reading books such as *Yatandou* by Gloria Whelan or Deborah Wiles' *Freedom Summer*. Students read with intent and purpose when they know they are going to write a response. They think more deeply about characters' actions and the consequences of those actions. Their understandings and connections to the text are heightened. And because of all of this, they are eager to read more literature.

The Lessons

This book offers teachers detailed lessons on how to guide students into a variety of literature responses. The first chapter addresses the text-to-self, text-to-text, and text-to-world connections. These are called personal connections because the reader makes his/her own link between the two based on personal experiences. In many schools, these three responses are the bread and butter of the primary grades. By the middle grades, standards place more importance on the key story elements of character, setting, conflict (plot), and theme. The greater part of this book provides detailed examples and instruction for story element responses.

Each lesson begins with an explanation of a particular response and proceeds through an introduction of the lesson, the classroom use of overhead samples, a writing plan, and composing the response. The section called "Another Look" provides reinforcement lessons with additional overhead samples from different books. Each chapter will enable language arts instructors to present substantive lessons that result in thoughtful, well-developed responses.

Short or Long? One Paragraph or More?

Writing literature responses needs to be a seamless part of the language arts program. Ideally, students will be writing responses throughout the year. We know that we want students responding to literature on a regular basis to develop their critical reading, thinking, and writing skills. Literature response is not a short unit of study we offer for a few weeks and then move on. It is an integral way of thinking for growing readers and writers.

Sometimes when I visit middle grade classrooms, teachers insist that literature responses be a set length, typically four to six major paragraphs. Students often learn to dislike the term *literature response* because they find the task of gathering enough information for a lengthy response overwhelming. I prefer that students write many small, focused responses of eight to fourteen sentences or so, rather than a few lengthy responses.

I know that many teachers like to divide all writing into a set number of paragraphs. With literature responses, I let that be a student choice. They can write three paragraphs—one for the lead, one for the middle, and one for the ending—but they can also write the entire response as one long paragraph. You'll notice on the overhead samples that I have a mixture of both.

If students organize their thoughts before they write, the response will usually follow that order. I want to place as much responsibility as possible on the student for selecting the kind of response, format, and supporting evidence, and for requesting feedback.

Evaluation

Each response is its own evaluation. If students are regularly engaged in thinking about and discussing what they read, the responses will improve in depth and quality as the year progresses. However, I do understand that sometimes teachers need to take a grade.

I have included two sample rubrics near the end of each chapter for that purpose, but feel free to create your own rubric for the responses. Better yet, allow students to help decide what criteria need to be on a particular response rubric. Please, though, make the rubric available to the students before they write, because then it will have a three-fold purpose:

- a goal setter
- a revision tool
- a form of evaluation

I have included a blank rubric at the end of this introduction for your convenience, and there is a corresponding transparency on Overhead 20. Feel free to reproduce it to use as you and your students create your own rubrics for the responses.

Audience

Audience feedback is an important part of the writing process. If we want to encourage students to be committed writers who express themselves with the strongest craft, then we need to provide time for them to receive specific feedback. We can manage audience time in a way that offers the most benefits. Since literature responses are an integral part of the language arts program, and students will be writing them often, feedback needs to be highly focused. Most audience feedback will happen in the classroom.

One of the most immediate ways for writers to receive authentic feedback is when it comes after the completion of the response. Before student writers share their work with a partner, they need to decide on a focus and ask the partner to listen specifically for that focus. Here are some questions writers may pose to their audiences to focus their feedback:

- *Is my response focused? Does it stick to my topic?*
- *Is my writing fluent? Does one sentence flow into another? Are there places where my writing sounds choppy or abrupt?*
- *Is my topic clear once I read the lead?*
- *Do I support my response well with examples from the book?*
- *What is your favorite phrase or sentence in this response? Why?*
- *What do you think is interesting about my ending?*
- *Do you agree with what I wrote? Do you disagree? Why?*

After asking a question, the writer reads the literature response and then asks the listener the question again at the end of the reading.

Listeners who have a purpose for listening are more attentive, so you might consider having the writer read the response two times. The first reading provides the listener with a general overview of the response. During the second reading, the listener can focus on the specific feature requested by the writer. The listener gives specific feedback, and then students switch roles.

The feedback students receive helps them refine their writing and increases their commitment to future writing. If students are writing for an authentic purpose and audience, they invest more time and thought and produce better writing. When students grow as writers, they want to become even better by writing more. It's a cycle that we just don't want to interrupt.

Literature

As you read through this book, you will notice that I have included many of the same titles in the different lessons. This is a direct result of conversations I have had with classroom teachers who have told me that due to limitations on time and funding, they find it easier to collect or purchase a few good books for day-to-day modeling. Here is a short list of some of the books that I use repeatedly to teach the writing of literature responses:

- *Across the Blue Pacific* by Louise Borden
- *Akiak* by Robert J. Blake
- *On My Honor* by Marion Dane Bauer
- *Rudi's Pond* by Eve Bunting
- *Scaredy Squirrel* by Melanie Watt
- *When Marian Sang* by Pam Muñoz Ryan

- *The White Elephant* by Sid Fleischman
- *Yatandou* by Gloria Whelan

Pick and choose the lessons from this book that complement your language arts program. Provide solid support for the students through your introductory lessons, your modeling, and your celebration of their good writing. With this kind of structure and encouragement, every response will be a success!

Rubric Form

	Excellent	Satisfactory	Needs Work

CHAPTER 1

Personal Connection Responses

THE QUESTION TO EXPLORE

What Is Personal Connection?

Personal connection is the most natural of reactions. We read a poem, a story, a work of narrative nonfiction, and we think to ourselves, *I agree with this*, or *I remember another story with a similar theme of a hard-working character.* Reading is thinking, reflecting, remembering, and making connections. At first we make *text-to-self* connections. We see ourselves somewhere in the pages we read—if not ourselves, our friends, families, beliefs, or interests.

As we grow more proficient as readers, we go beyond making personal connections with literature. The more we read, the more we see the similarities and differences between storylines, author styles, presentation of information, and genre structures. We build new understandings about how authors and illustrators use their craft to engage us on a new level. In these *text-to-text* responses, readers compare a feature of text between two or more stories, poems, or works of nonfiction.

As we continue to read and think more deeply about the written word, an even bigger picture emerges. In *text-to-world* responses, readers connect an important feature of the work—a theme, certain information, or a character struggle—to a condition or truth that they have come to appreciate in the world around them. It is at this level of reading and thinking that readers become part of the universal bond that ties all of humankind together through literature.

Why Teach Personal Connection Responses?

Children understand what they read better when they find it engaging, so we encourage the youngest readers to think about what they read. That's why many primary-age readers regularly write literature responses: to increase their comprehension of what they read. It also makes them want to read more.

We teach personal connection responses because we want to create stronger, more thoughtful readers, who, in turn, become more critical readers. But there is another purpose to all of this. As readers think more deeply about text, they learn more about others and themselves. The reader becomes actively involved with the human experience.

Introducing Personal Connections

Start with a discussion that centers around a story that is well-known to all of your students. I use "The Three Little Pigs" for this introductory lesson, but you could substitute any story that your students have recently enjoyed.

Teacher: Remember the story of "The Three Little Pigs"? Could one of you please summarize what happens in that story? (*Provide time for one or two students to share the key scenes from the story.*)

Now, I want you to think about this story for a moment. Did anything happen in this story that reminds you of a time when you had to work with others? Or perhaps it reminds you of a time when you hurriedly put something together, only to have to redo it later. Does it remind you of something you once made with a brother or sister? Have you ever worked with your family to make your house better in some way?

Provide time for students to reflect. Eventually a hand or two will go up, and students will start sharing stories that for one reason or another are similar to "The Three Little Pigs." If during their explanations they forget to tie their experience to the story, guide them with questions to help them do that. For instance, you might ask:

- *How did the story remind you of that?*
- *Which part of the story is similar to what you experienced?*
- *Which character in the story reminds you of that person?*

Teacher: Sometimes when we read a story, we make a personal connection to an event, a person, or something in that story. It makes a deep impression on us, and we remember something from our own lives quite vividly. This is called a *text-to-self*

Lesson Commentary

Depending on your students' past reading/writing programs, many will be familiar with text-to-self connections.

connection. When we can relate to the text, it gives new importance and meaning to what we are reading, and we engage more actively in the story, poem, or information. In other words, it means more to us.

I saw that many of you did not have a personal connection to "The Three Little Pigs." That's to be expected. Not every story will have the same impact on all of us.

I have another question. Did the story of "The Three Little Pigs" remind you of any other book you have read recently or in the past? Can you think of a story where brothers worked together? Can you think of a story where someone out-tricked a fox or wolf or another enemy? Can you think of another story where in the end the bad animal or enemy ends up in a kettle or in the fire, or being hurt?

Allow time for student responses. For instance, someone might tell you that the ending of "The Three Little Pigs" reminds him of the ending of "Little Red Riding Hood," when the woodcutter opens the wolf and takes out Granny. Both end with the naughty animal dead and gone. Another child might mention that at the end of "Hansel and Gretel," the mean old witch ends up in the oven because Gretel outwits her. If the students cannot think of any text-to-text connections, you can offer some titles of recently read books that provide possibilities.

Teacher: When we can find similarities between two or more stories or books, it is called a *text-to-text* connection. It simply means that you notice similar events, characters, or themes between stories.

But there is one more kind of connection. So let me ask you another question about "The Three Little Pigs." Does anything happen in that story that reminds you of something in the world? Does the collaboration between brothers remind you of anything? Does the big bad wolf huffing and puffing remind you of anything else? Does the image of little guys fighting off a much bigger guy remind you of anything?

Student responses will really depend on how much they read and think about the outside world. For instance, someone may remark that sports teams pull together and strategize to beat their opponents, just like the three little pigs did. Or someone may comment that severe weather is like the big bad wolf. We know it's coming and it makes a lot of noise, but if people are prepared, they can withstand its fury. Or another student might say that little businessmen are like the three little pigs and big businesses are like the big bad wolf. If the students have had practice with this kind of process in past years, it will come easier. If they have not, you will need to prime them with a few examples.

Teacher: Thank you for your thoughts. When we compare some aspect of the story to what's going on somewhere in the world, it is called a *text-to-world* connection. We will be writing a few of these literature responses this year so we can see how literature connects to what is happening in our world. We will explore how events and people in books and those in real life are quite similar. Let's practice so we can easily write about the connections that are the strongest for us.

How Can We Help Students Make Connections?

To guide students to make connections, I begin with a read-aloud and model how I make connections to the story. Then I invite students to do the same, in a lesson that goes something like the following exchange.

Teacher: I'm going to read the book *Granddad's Fishing Buddy* by Mary Quigley. This is a book about a man and his granddaughter fishing on a lake in the morning.

Even if you've never fished in your life, you must have shared a special time with a grandfather, a grandmother, an uncle, or a neighbor. We all have fond memories of spending time with someone who cares for us. Perhaps you baked cookies with a grandmother or ice-skated with an uncle. Or maybe a neighbor took you to play miniature golf.

If you do fish, I'm sure some of the images in this story will remind you of what you've seen, heard or felt while fishing yourself.

When I was in fourth and fifth grade, I used to go fishing with our neighbor, Mr. Dewitt. In fact, he taught me how to fish. When I first read this story, it reminded me of how patient and kind Mr. Dewitt was when helping me with the bait and hook.

Listen to the story and enjoy!

Read the book and then continue with the discussion by asking if anyone has a personal connection to the story.

Students will have quite a few stories. Listen to three or four, then, tell the students to turn to a partner and share their personal connection with this story. Allow two to three minutes for students to share. When everyone has finished, continue the lesson.

Teacher: Now, think of the one image, scene, or piece of dialogue that made you think of something in your life. We can call that a trigger. When you read a poem, story, or work of nonfiction, and some part of it grabs you and you connect to it, that passage is your trigger.

Now, we're ready to learn how to plan and write our personal connection responses.

If you have additional time, you can proceed with the next part of the lesson. If not, this is natural stopping point.

How Can We Guide Students to Write Their Responses?

If you're picking up the lesson on another day, begin with a quick review. Ask the students to describe a personal connection they have made to literature, either through discussion or by writing a brief description in their writer's notebooks. Have them name the three different kinds of personal connections—text-to-self, text-to-text, and text-to-world—then continue the lesson.

Teacher: When we read something that touches us or makes us think deeply, or reminds us of another book or character, or something similar in the world, we can write about it. We call this a literature response.

I'm going to show you a text-to-self literature response for *Granddad's Fishing Buddy*.

Place Personal Connection Sample 1 (Overhead 1) on the overhead projector and read it aloud twice to the students.

Teacher: Where do you first see the title of the book and the author's name?

Student: In the first sentence.

Teacher: Yes. We always put the title and author's name somewhere in the lead of the response. Would you please come up here and underline both of those with the blue marker?

Where does the writer first mention that he had a connection with the story?

Student: When he writes, "This story reminded me of fishing with my father."

Teacher: Right. Please come up and underline that sentence in green.

Now, this will take a little rereading, but how many different details did this writer share? In other words, did the writer only mention one thing about fishing with his dad, or were there more?

Students will say that there was more than one detail. They'll read and count, and most will come to the conclusion that there are three different details. Ask a different student to underline each of the details.

Students will mention the following kinds of details:

- how the author's term "glassy lake" reminded the writer of how smooth the lake was when he was fishing
- how the scene when the grandfather is putting a worm on his hook

Lesson Commentary

The purpose of examining a sample literature response is to draw the students' attention to the different components. This will help them plan their own brief responses. The more familiar they are with the features of a well-written response, the more carryover you will see in their written work.

reminds the writer that he was initially hesitant about putting the worm on his hook, but eventually was able to do it

- how the heron landing in the lily pads reminded the writer how he and his dad would row into the lily pads and drift before dropping the anchor

Teacher: You all did a great job of finding three details in this connection response. I have one more question. In the ending, did the writer only mention the details from earlier in the piece, or are there different ones?

Student: They are different—the gentle days, the heat of the sun, and the pull of the pole.

Teacher: Strong writers add a new thought to put in their endings—something they have not said earlier in the piece. Of course, the new information or ideas need to relate to their topic. That's what keeps the writing focused.

Thank you for your careful reading and thinking. Now, I'd like to help you plan your own personal response to this book.

Continue the lesson if time permits. Otherwise, keep this overhead with the underlined phrases available for the next day's lesson. In the next part of the lesson, you'll model how to plan a personal connection, writing your notes on a blank transparency so students can see the whole process.

Before you continue, ask all of the students if they have a strong personal connection to this story. If not, allow them to write a personal connection literature response for another story to which they do have a connection.

Teacher: All of us, including me, are now going to plan our own personal connection responses to the story *Granddad's Fishing Buddy*. Let's begin.

Place an *L* at the top of your paper like this. (*Write an L on the transparency.*)

This *L* stands for the lead. Now, let's decide what information needs to be in our lead. What did we underline in the lead of the transparency? The lead is the first two sentences of the personal connection response.

Student: We underlined the title, the author's name, and "This story reminded me of fishing with my father."

Teacher: Yes. We need to have all three of those things in our lead: title, author, and our connection. Let's add the title and author to our plans. (*Write on transparency.*) Now, we need to think about the connection. We don't want to just copy what the writer of the overhead wrote. Some of you do have your own fishing connections, and you certainly can write about those. But some of us are going to write about doing something special with a person

L

L

Title—Granddad's Fishing
       Buddy

Author—Mary Quigley

Text-to-self Con.—
       gardening—
       Uncle Louis

L

Title—Granddad's Fishing
       Buddy

Author—Mary Quigley

Text-to-self Con.—
       gardening—
       Uncle Louis

M

U. L. going outside—
       I tag along

who cares for us. Some of us might write about how this story reminds us of another activity in the quiet of early morning. Others might be inspired to write about something besides fishing that they like to do outside in nature. Let's take a few moments to decide what our connection is to this story. (*Pause.*)

I've decided to write about gardening with my Uncle Louis. Sara in this story was learning to fish with her grandfather, and I learned to garden with my Uncle Louis. So I'm going to add a brief note to my plan to remind me of my focus.

I'd like to hear what some of your connections are before we continue.

Students will have a variety of connections. Sharing them aloud will help the students who are struggling to find a connection.

Teacher: Write a brief note about your connection on your plan.

Now I'd like you to add an *M* on your plan, like this. *M* stands for the middle of your response.

The writer of the response that we studied had three different details in the connection. Three is a good number for the middle. It's our goal. But if you can only think of two details, that will be fine for your first attempt.

Let's spend a moment and think about something that was said or happened in *Granddad's Fishing Buddy* and how that relates to our connection and what details we want to mention. (*Pause.*)

I have my first detail. I'm going to write it as a brief note; you do the same. Think of something in your experience that is similar to this story. (*Write first detail note on transparency.*) I have another one. Take a moment or two and think about something that happens or is said in this story and how that reminds you of another detail.

Circulate around the room as students are adding their details. Make sure these are hearty details that they can expand in their writing. And make sure the details stay focused on students' connections. After most students have written their details, ask for volunteers to share their plans. A few students are usually delighted to read their plans. It helps writers get some feedback for their ideas, and it helps students who may be struggling to think of something to write.

Teacher: We are now ready for a third detail, if you can think of one. I know that I have another detail. I'll go ahead and add it to my plan as you think of your third one.

Circulate around the room as students continue their plans. Celebrate when you see someone adding details that are relevant. Nudge those who may be struggling with questions about their connection. Afterward, provide a few minutes to hear three or four plans in their entirety.

Teacher: I'm proud of how you all are staying focused on your connection and finding some good details to add interest.

Let's plan our endings. You can start by adding an *E* to the bottom of your plans.

In the sample response, we noted that the ending mentioned a few new details. It also had a final sentence that pulled the response together. Let's think about how we want to end our responses. When I have an idea, I'll write it on my plan. When you know what you want to write, add a note to your plans.

I thought of what I want to say in my ending; have you? As soon as you decide, please add it to your plans.

Circulate around the room, praising the efforts of students who are planning well and nudging others who may be struggling by posing questions about their connection.

After plans are complete, ask for volunteers to share their entire plans. Provide time for two or three students to share with the whole group. Then have students quickly share their plans with a partner. This sharing can have two benefits. Students who listen generally ask questions that help the writer flesh out details, and the writer becomes more committed to writing the response because someone has shown interest in his or her plan.

If you have time, continue with the modeling of how to compose this response from the plan. If you need to stop at this point, make sure your students store their plans in a safe place until you can resume the lesson.

L

Title—<u>Granddad's Fishing Buddy</u>

Author—Mary Quigley

Text-to-self Con.— gardening— Uncle Louis

M

1. U. L. going outside— I tag along

2. I did best to imitate

3. pick tomatoes, dig potatoes

E

learned a lot about planting, harvesting, and pruning

what we shared— lifetime

Written Plans vs. Mental Plans ❋

Your students do not need a written plan for every response they write, but it is a good tool to demonstrate and model. For the child who has difficulty with organizing ideas mentally, the written plan provides a framework for the writing. Some students can plan mentally and include all of their details in an organized manner. If a student proves that he can do mental prewriting, it is not necessary to demand a written plan for every response. I do suggest that you require a written plan when introducing a new kind of response. After the initial attempt, it's up to you to let each student decide on his or her individual process.

Composing the Personal Connection Response

L

Title—<u>Granddad's Fishing Buddy</u>

Author—Mary Quigley

Text-to-self Con.—
       gardening—
       Uncle Louis

If you are resuming this lesson on a new day, make sure you provide time for each student to read his or her plan to a writing buddy. This will help them remember their ideas and mentally prepare them for the writing.

Display your plan so all students can see it. Point to the information you have written for your lead.

Model how to draft a lead of one to three sentences for students. A lead for this plan might look like this:

As I was reading <u>Granddad's Fishing Buddy</u> by Mary Quigley, and enjoying the relationship between Sara and her grandfather, I remembered my Uncle Louis. Every year I would visit him and Grandma in Massachusetts. He had a huge garden and was always happy to show his great niece—me—anything I wanted to know.

Ask the students:

- *Do I have the title of the book?*
- *Do I have the author's name?*
- *Have I stated a connection?*

Students should be able to identify each of the criteria.

Teacher: I'm glad that I was able to place all three pieces of necessary information into my lead. That is what I would like you to do now. Make sure to write all of the information on your plan for your lead. You might add one small interesting detail, as long as it's not from your middle choices, for extra appeal.

Walk around the classroom, posing questions and responding positively to any solid or unique leads. If a child is laboring, point to the information on his or her lead plan and ask a question or two to launch the student into independent writing. When most of the students have completed their leads, give them a moment to reread and revise. Then ask for two or three volunteers to share their leads with the class, and provide time for positive feedback.

Next, point to your plan and all of the information under the M.

Discuss how you would like to begin, then write your middle as an example. For this plan, the writing might look something like this:

M

1. U. L. going outside—
     I tag along

2. I did best to imitate

3. pick tomatoes,
     dig potatoes

Uncle Louis kept his gardening clothes and tools on the back porch of Grandma's house. When I would see him getting ready to go outside, I would ask if I could help him. With a twinkle in his eye, he'd say, "Sure, but you know you're going to get dirty." I didn't care. I'd do my best to imitate him when he cultivated in the rows or tied up the pole beans. Standing right beside him, I'd follow his every move. My two favorite activities in July were picking the many tomatoes and digging up the new potatoes. They weren't very big, but they were tasty.

Before asking students to write, give them an opportunity to discuss how you have stretched your details from your plan to the writing. Have them find all three of the details in your middle, and ask them if you are staying focused on your connection. Note that the details in this version all come from personal experience, not from the book, and that's okay for this type of response. Then remind them to do the same—stretch out their details and stay focused on their connection—as they flesh out the middle of their responses.

Walk through the classroom as they write, pointing out well-developed details and focused writing. If students are struggling, prompt them with questions about their connection and plan.

When most students have completed this part of the response, ask again for volunteers to read their leads and middles. Provide time for the class to offer specific positive feedback.

Next, mention the ending of your plan. Model how to draft a concise ending (one to three sentences) that matches your note. For this plan, it might read something like this:

Over the eighteen summers I worked with Uncle Louis, I learned quite a bit about planting seeds and young seedlings, harvesting fruit and vegetables, and pruning plants to keep them healthy. And just like Sara learned lessons about fishing, I learned a lot about gardening that has lasted me a lifetime.

Ask the students to look at the notes they wrote in their own plans for their endings. Provide time for them to draft. Circulate among them and provide feedback. When they've completed their endings, ask for a few volunteers to share their endings or their entire responses.

Audience

Remember to give students an opportunity to share their final responses with one another, either with partners or in small groups. Every writer appreciates specific feedback. This does not have to be a lengthy investment of time; partner sharing with feedback may only take five minutes or so. Refer to the introduction of this book for additional ideas on how writers can request feedback from a listener. Receiving feedback is an essential part of the writing process that spurs students to write again.

TRANSPARENCY

E

learned a lot about planting, harvesting, and pruning

what we shared—lifetime

GRADING OF A PERSONAL CONNECTION RESPONSE

It is not necessary to grade every response. However, if you feel a grade is needed, use a simple rubric and discuss it with students before they write their responses. Make sure your evaluations are based solely on the listed criteria. Following are two rubrics that you might use for personal connections.

Personal Connection Responses

RUBRIC 1

	Excellent	Satisfactory	Needs Work
Lead	Includes title, author, and connection	Includes two of three lead elements	Includes one or none of the lead elements
Vocabulary	Includes at least seven specific terms or phrases	Includes five or six specific terms or phrases	Includes four or fewer specific terms or phrases
Voice	Writing has a distinct writer's voice	Some of the writing has a distinct writer's voice	Little or none of the writing has a distinct voice

RUBRIC 2

	Excellent	Satisfactory	Needs Work
Lead	Includes title, author, and connection	Includes two of the three lead elements	Includes one or none of the lead elements
Middle	Elaborates on three or more details of the writer's connection	Elaborates on two details of the writer's connection	Lists 2–3 simple details or words, or elaborates on one detail of the writer's connection
Focus	Writing is focused on the writer's connection	Most of the writing is focused on the writer's connection	Little or none of the writing is focused on the writer's connection

Lesson Review

1. Discuss personal connections to literature.

2. Introduce the *text-to-self, text-to-text,* and *text-to-world* connections.

3. Read a familiar story with which students will likely make strong connections.

4. Study a sample of a personal connection response and identify key components.

5. Create a simple plan for a lead, middle, and end.

6. Compose a personal connection response using the plan as a guide.

7. Invite students to share with an audience and receive feedback on what they did well.

Another Look

Reinforcement Lesson for Text-to-Text Response

Text-to-text responses are typically written to compare one aspect of a poem, story, or piece of nonfiction with another literary work. The comparison might focus on theme, character, setting, conflict, style of writing, content topic, or another feature of the text. To demonstrate this kind of response, make sure that students have recently read some literary works with similar features. Then have them study the Personal Connection Sample 2 (Overhead 2). Follow the same steps as you did for the lesson on text-to-self, except that in the middle of this response, write a detailed comparison of the one feature that is the focus of the response.

Reinforcement Lesson for Text-to-World Response

Text-to-world responses are dependent on the students' knowledge and experiences. I would never recommend asking all students to write a text-to-world response, but I do suggest that all students be taught how to write one. When and if they read a text and make this type of connection, they will have the background to organize and proceed. To demonstrate this kind of response, go through the same steps as shown in the lesson on text-to-self at the beginning of this chapter, using the Personal Connection Sample 3 (Overhead 3). Instead of having every child write this response, write one collaboratively.

The Best Literature for Personal Connections

In subsequent chapters, I recommend books for the various responses, but for personal connections, I believe it's better for students to identify literature from their regular reading that will launch them into writing these responses. The connection needs to be authentic, with the writer discovering a personal purpose for writing that grows from an understanding or memory.

OVERHEAD 1   **1**   ## Granddad's Fishing Buddy (Text-to-Self)

In the book *Granddad's Fishing Buddy* by Mary Quigley, the author describes in great detail the first fishing experience of Sara, a young girl. This story reminded me of fishing with my father.

When the author refers to the water as a "glassy lake," I remember looking out over the water, thinking it was so smooth and shiny, that if I was very careful I would be able to get out of the boat and walk across it.

There's a scene where her grandfather is putting the worm on his hook. Unlike Sara, I didn't have any licorice to put on my hook, but I was hesitant. However, I was strong-willed and not about to let anyone else do it for me. So, little by little, I learned how to take my nightcrawler and loop it around and on the hook.

I could also relate to the heron landing in the lily pads. Most of the time when we fished, my dad would row the boat into the lily pads, let it drift a bit, and then ask me to drop the anchor. We would throw our lines out from the lake flowers and hope that fish were hungry.

Reading this book brought back lots of great memories—thoughts of gentle days, the heat of the sun and the pull on the pole when a fish nibbled. A day spent on the lake with my father was a great treat.

OVERHEAD 2   **2**   ## Rudi's Pond and On My Honor (Text-to-Text)

In both of these books, *Rudi's Pond* by Eve Bunting and *On My Honor* by Marion Dane Bauer, a childhood friend dies. No matter what age, it's always tragic to lose a friend to death, and these authors show two completely different reactions.

In *Rudi's Pond*, the narrator knows that Rudi has been ill. Even though she has seen him in bed for several days at a time and knows he has gone to the hospital, she is still shocked when he is gone forever. But she comforts herself with an object that they made together. She remembers him fondly and knows that a part of him will always be with her.

In *On My Honor*, Joel's friend Tony was never ill. He was a robust young teen who was always up for a new adventure. His death was unannounced and caused by an accident. Since the boys were together at the time of Tony's death, Joel assumed some responsibility for his drowning. Initially, he couldn't even grieve properly for his friend because his guilt was all-consuming.

These two stories offer two perspectives on how to handle death. *Rudi's Pond* is all about a young child accepting the unfair death of a friend. *On My Honor* explores how a conscientious boy deals with the circumstances surrounding the death of his best friend while they are together. There are some common threads in both stories, though. The narrator and Joel go through some of the same feelings when they realize what has happened. They both feel a huge personal loss. They cannot accept the death as real, and they struggle to come to terms with it.

Overheads—Personal Connections

OVERHEAD 3 (3) Scaredy Squirrel (Text-to-World)

Scaredy Squirrel is in a rut in the book *Scaredy Squirrel* by Melanie Watt. He never leaves his nut tree—never. He wants to be safe. And, he has a plan for just about everything, including hazards that shouldn't even be a consideration for a squirrel, like sharks and green Martians.

I think many of us live our lives this way. Once we establish a routine and nothing bad happens, we maintain those habits day in and out. I know married couples who do the same things on the same days of the week with absolutely no change in their schedules. The only time they break their routine is for the holidays for a few hours or days.

Consider the laws that govern states of the nation. People abide by them, enforce them, even if conditions drastically change from the time they were put into law. To change a law or enact a new law takes time and much work.

Some individuals drive the same streets to work and home every day. They stop at the same stores and get gas for their vehicles at the same gas stations.

Personally, I like a small amount of change in my life every day. That's how I have new experiences and learn. I don't think we should be like Scaredy Squirrel. A little adventure just might open our eyes to new possibilities.

CHAPTER 2

Character Response

What Is Character?

In a story, characters drive the action. The protagonist is the main character—the person (or animal or thing) who needs or wants something. The antagonist is the character who tries to prevent the protagonist from reaching that goal. Supporting characters either help or hinder the protagonist.

All characters have traits that guide their choices and actions. A brave character is likely to risk his or her own safety for the good of others. An honest character will dig out the truth at all costs. A resourceful character will use anything and everything in his or her power to accomplish a goal, and often does so quite cleverly. A selfish character will try to manipulate the actions of others to serve himself. A dishonorable character will attempt to take credit for the honorable actions of others.

But no character is all good or all bad. Just as in real life, characters in books are a blend of traits. In fact, if they weren't a blend, it would be difficult for readers to relate to them. For this reason, authors do their best to create protagonists who readers recognize. They act like us. They have doubts and fears like us. They work hard and struggle with problems. These characters represent the best and worst of us. It is through these characters that authors portray the shared humanity that exists between all people and across time.

When students write a character response, they examine different characters carefully. They see how these fictional or real people respond to conflict, overcome challenges, and cope with change or disaster. And since students often relate to these protagonists, they watch for ways they can handle similar struggles and obstacles in their own lives. In this way, writing character responses not only extends students' critical thinking skills, it also offers an opportunity to reflect on how they can use their strengths and talents to change and grow.

Why Teach Character Response?

Since characters are at the center of every story, we focus on character in the first literature responses we demonstrate for middle-grade students. We want them to be more critical readers, which entails understanding characters and how they behave. Readers learn the traits of characters by observing and considering what they do and the words they speak. A good story will never come out and say "the pirate was sentimental." Instead, it will show the trait by what he does, says, and thinks.

In their story writing, students learn how to craft believable characters by examining the work of published authors. They put into practice what they learn from careful reading and responding. To help them become stronger readers and writers, we need to encourage our students to take a careful look at the characters in the books they read.

Introducing Character

Start by generating a list of character traits, so students get a clear idea of what one is. Then move into a discussion of traits of well-known characters.

Teacher: I would like us to make a list of character traits. Let's think of some positive and negative qualities that a real-life person or book character might possess. For instance, a person or character could be curious or helpful. What are some other character traits we can add to our list?

Write the words *curious* and *helpful* on a transparency or on the white board, and record student responses as well. You may need to give them a few more examples to get them started. A completed list might look like this:

curious	helpful	shy	resourceful	determined
organized	impulsive	whimsical	playful	honest
brave	selfless	rebellious	considerate	kind
lazy	vengeful	gracious	compassionate	secretive
loving	wise	selfish	athletic	talented
strong	cooperative	humorous	inventive	disrespectful

Teacher: This is a great list. Now let's think a little bit deeper about character in a story, and how actions and words reveal a character's traits. I'm going to name some well-known characters, and you tell me one trait that you think fits them. The first character is Templeton the rat in *Charlotte's Web*. What characteristic do you think describes him?

Student: Sneaky and smart-aleck.

Student: Templeton is selfish.

Teacher: I agree with those choices. Let's try another character. How would you describe Cinderella?

Student: Hard-working.

Student: She was lonely.

Student: Cinderella was kind and helpful.

Teacher: Again, I agree with your choices. Now this time I want you to tell me a trait that describes this character and the reason that you've chosen it. For instance, if you told me that Templeton was selfish, you might mention how he was always asking what he would get if he did something for another animal. Or if you mentioned that he was greedy, you would remind us how he hoarded food so no one else could get it.

Okay, think of a trait for the giant in Jack and the Beanstalk and be ready to tell the reason you chose it.

Student: The giant was greedy because every morning he got out all of his gold coins and counted them again and again.

Student: The giant was demanding because he always wanted everything the same and only the food that he ordered.

Student: The giant was lazy because he ordered someone else to do all of his work.

Teacher: You're doing a great job with this. I would now like you to tell me a trait for a character and give me two specific examples from the story that support your description. The character I would like you to describe with a trait is _____. (*Name the protagonist of a middle-grade novel that your class has recently read.*)

If you select a recent title, students will be able to name a trait and support it with two different actions or conversations from the novel. Once students have explored the idea of character traits in this manner, they are ready to move on to writing character literature responses.

THE LESSON–PART 1

How Can We Help Students Identify Character Traits?

Always begin by reading a short story to the students that they have heard or read at least once before. It's essential that students are familiar with a story before examining the different story features. Since it is easier to introduce and practice literature responses with picture books or short stories, I like to use the book *The White Elephant* by Sid Fleischman.

Before you reread the story, tell the students what you enjoy about this title.

Teacher: I've always been fascinated with elephants, especially their loyalties to their owners. This story took me into Siam of long ago and showed me the love between man and animal. I know all of you probably remember this story, but I'd like to read it again. While I'm reading, think about the three main characters: Run-Run, Walking Mountain, and Sahib.

Feel free to jot down any traits that you think describe these characters. Think about their actions or about what Run-Run says for ways to describe them.

Read the book aloud to the students. This story takes a while to read, so you might have to end your lesson here and resume tomorrow. If time permits, continue by putting a clean transparency on the overhead projector and recording character traits for the three main characters in the book.

Teacher: We are going to make a few notes for all three characters in this book. Let's begin with Run-Run. (*Write* Run-Run *on the overhead transparency.*) What traits do you think describe Run-Run?

Answers will vary. Make sure you only write those that are traits; do not write physical descriptions of the boy. Some of the responses might be: *conscientious, honest, loving, kind, clever.*

Teacher: What about Run-Run's original elephant, Walking Mountain? What traits do you think describe him?

Sample responses might include: *loyal, hard-working, jealous, protective, brave.*

Teacher: Let's add Sahib to this list. What traits do you think describe him? As you can see, sometimes certain traits appear at different places in the story.

Responses may include: *spoiled, attentive, loyal, strong, adaptive.*

Teacher: This is a great list. It will help us later when we write our own character literature response. But right now, I'd like to show you what a completed character response looks like.

If you have additional time, proceed with the next part of the lesson. If you need to stop here for the day, keep the list of traits for the next time you return to it.

THE LESSON–PART 2

How Can We Guide Students to Write Their Responses?

If you're picking up the lesson on another day, begin by asking a student to briefly summarize *The White Elephant*. Then place the list of traits that the class developed on the overhead projector so everyone can see it. As another quick refresher, ask students to tell you the two main ways that a reader comes to understand a character in a story. Hopefully they will remember that it is through the character's actions and words.

Teacher: Thinking and writing about character is interesting and fun. It's like being a detective and finding clues in the text to discover who a character really is. Today I'd like each of you to plan a brief literature response about one of the characters from *The White Elephant*. But first, let's examine a character literature response so we know how to present our thoughts.

Place Character Sample 1 (Overhead 4) on the overhead projector and read it aloud twice.

Teacher: Where do you first see the title of the book and the author's name?

Student: They're both in the first sentence.

Teacher: Yes. We always put the title and author's name somewhere in the lead of the response. Would you please come up and underline both of those with blue marker?
Where does this writer first mention the word *character*?

Student: In the beginning of the second sentence.

Teacher: Yes. Again, we always want to include the word *character* somewhere in the lead so our audience knows what kind of response is being written. Would you please come up and underline that word in green?
In this response, what is the one trait that the writer is going to support with examples from the story?

Some students might say that he has little food and no luxuries, but others will know that the trait is generosity.

Teacher: Yes, generosity is the trait. Let's underline that in black. This is the focus of the response. The writer now needs to show us through specific examples from the story that Run-Run was generous. As we find examples, we'll underline them in black.
Okay, can you locate an example of Run-Run's generosity?

Repeat this process until the students have underlined at least four examples of his generosity. Examples include sharing the watermelon and rinds; asking Walking Mountain to accept Sahib; sharing his meager food supply with Sahib and not punishing him for raiding it; preparing Sahib for the Prince's mahout and his departure; and coaxing Sahib to obey the mahout's orders.

Teacher: Is the word *generous* repeated in the ending?

Student: Yes, it's in the first line of the ending.

Teacher: Right. It is a good idea to repeat the trait at the end and write how it had an impact on the story.

Nice job identifying the important parts of this literature response. Now we are ready to write our own.

Continue with this lesson if you have time. If you need to stop for the day, keep the overhead with the items they have underlined available for the next day's lesson. You'll need a clean transparency to model the planning process.

Teacher: All of us, including me, are now going to plan our own character literature responses for this story. Let's begin.

Place an *L* at the top of your paper.

This *L* stands for the lead. What did we underline in this character literature response?

Student: The title, the author's name, the word *character*, and the trait that was the focus.

Teacher: Good. Let's add those items, one by one, to our own plans, starting with the title. Write a *T* and then the title on your plans.

Now add an *A* for author and write his name. I'll do the same on mine.

At this point, you need to decide on which of the three characters you'd like to focus with your response. Would you like to talk about a trait of Run-Run, Walking Mountain, or Sahib? You might also decide on the trait right now, so you can think about the story and make sure you'll have enough support for your response. I'm going to think about this, too. (*After a few moments, write* Trait—persistence *on the transparency.*)

As you can see, I've decided to write about Sahib and his persistence. Let's take another moment and make sure we have all of the information for the lead that we need.

This is a good time to circulate through the room, celebrating good examples of the characters and traits chosen by the students and supporting those students who may be struggling. You might decide to stop and have a few students share their plans for their leads. It's a good way for students to see the diversity of possible responses. Only take time for three or four to briefly share, and then move on.

Teacher: I'm going to add an *M* on my plan for the middle and I'd like you to do that on your own plans.

The middle is where we show specific actions and words that demonstrate this trait in the story. We'll try to find four examples, but if you can only find three, that is a great start for today. Since this is a plan, only write a word or two to remind yourself of the scene that you want to write about in your response. Also, I have a

L
T—<u>The White Elephant</u>
A—Sid Fleischman
C—Sahib
Trait—persistence

few extra copies of the book up at the front of the room, so if you need to examine the story carefully to find support, please do. Just make sure to return the book so another student may use it.

At first, model by thinking aloud. This gives students an opportunity to see how you make a connection between the trait and specific actions or words from the text.

After you list your supporting examples, circulate through the room reading plans. Offer positive feedback to students who are finding strong support for their character trait and guidance to those who are struggling. Keep them focused by asking questions:

- *Which character did you select?*
- *Which trait do you think this character demonstrates in the story?*
- *What made you choose this trait?*
- *Do you remember a scene or something she said that made you think of this word?*
- *Are there other scenes where your character exhibits this trait?*
- *Do you need to examine a copy of the story?*

After most students have listed their supporting examples, ask a few to share everything on their plans from top to bottom. Provide time for students to comment on their supporting examples from the text.

L

T—The White Elephant
A—Sid Fleischman
C—Sahib
Trait—persistence

M

returned after peacock

kept breaking leg chain

wanted to dig trunks

attacked tiger twice

always nudging R-R

E

Sahib's pers. fused
friendship

Teacher: We've almost completed our plans. Having a plan makes the writing of the response easier and more enjoyable. Once you know what you want to say, you can concentrate on good word choice and organization.

Let's add an *E* to our plans for the ending. In the response we examined on the overhead, the ending mentioned how Run-Run's generosity affected him in the story. Stop and think for a moment. How does the trait you are focusing on affect your character, or the story, or both? I will be thinking of the same thing.

If you would like your ending to be personal, and you have a connection to this trait—either you exhibit it, or you know someone else who has this trait, you can briefly discuss that for your ending. For my response, I think I'll write about how Sahib's persistence fused a friendship.

Think about your choice and decide what you want to write.

Circulate again around the classroom and make sure everyone understands the task. Point out good examples of brevity. When you see someone jotting down just a few words, mention it. If you see someone connect their trait to the rest of the response, mention that, too. Keep highlighting what the students are doing well.

Teacher: We have time to listen to a few completed plans. Who would like to share?

Plan Together at First

It is not necessary to require a plan for every literature response that your students write during the year, but it is a good idea to model planning when introducing a new kind of response. It helps students organize their ideas and tells them right from the start that a brief, focused response is valued in your classroom. Some students will choose to create written plans in the future, and other students will organize their thoughts in their heads. In either case, students need to know that thinking and planning are always important in the writing process.

Provide time for three or four response plans and give positive feedback.

If you have time, model how to write this first literature response. If you need to stop for the day, make sure your students store their plans in a safe place until you can resume the lesson.

THE LESSON–PART 3

Composing the Character Response

If you are picking up this lesson on a new day, make sure you provide time for students to read their plans to a writing buddy. This helps students remember what they want to write about, and inspires partners to ask one or two questions that make writers go back and improve the plan. Again, students can either write the response as one long paragraph or if they're comfortable using paragraphs, they can divide it into the lead, middle, and ending. Still others might want to elaborate and create a separate paragraph for the lead, each middle point, and the ending.

Display your plan so all students can see it. Point to the information you have written for your lead. Then model how to draft a lead. It might look something like this:

> Sahib is the name of a character in Sid Fleischman's book <u>The White Elephant</u>. At first, he is unwanted, but because of his persistence, Sahib finds a place in Run-Run's stable, and in his heart.

Then, ask the students:

- *Do I have the author's name?* (yes)
- *Do I have the book's title?* (yes)
- *Do I have the word* character? (yes)
- *Do I mention one trait?* (yes)

Teacher: Good. I was able to place all four pieces of necessary information into my lead. That is what I would like you to do now. Make sure that all of the information on your plan for your lead is written so it makes sense. You might also add one small interesting detail to appeal to your reader.

Walk around the classroom, nudging with questions and celebrating any solid or unique leads. If a student is laboring, point to the information on his or her lead and ask a question or two to launch them into independent writing. When the students have completed their leads, give them a moment to reread and revise. Then ask for three or four volunteers to share their leads with the class, and provide time for positive feedback.

Next, point to your plan and all of the information under the M for middle. Discuss how you would like to begin and then write your middle as an example. It might look something like this:

M

returned after peacock

kept breaking leg chain

wanted to dig trunks

attacked tiger twice

always nudging R-R

Run-Run offers Sahib a couple of opportunities to be free and run away. Sahib leaves, but he always returns to the stable. After Sahib follows Run-Run and Walking Mountain to the fields where they are removing stumps, Run-Run shackles his leg at the stable. Because of his desire to be with them, Sahib persists until he is able to free himself and drag the chain and post to the field. Even though Sahib is not supposed to work, he repeatedly pushes the stumps and pulls them free. Since he is a strong worker and seems to enjoy the task, Run-Run gives in and covers him with mud so he is not recognizable as the white elephant. After witnessing Walking Mountain's attack on a tiger, Sahib saves the Prince by pitching a tiger with his tusks. But he doesn't stop with one attack. He is persistent and gores the tiger again. As the story progresses, Sahib continually nudges Run-Run playfully with his trunk. Eventually, Run-Run looks forward to those pushes and rolls and returns Sahib's affection.

Before asking the students to write, give them an opportunity to see how many specific references are in your middle. Then ask, "Do these examples show Sahib's persistence in the story?" If they say yes, tell them how pleased you are that you are staying focused in your response.

Guide students to examine their own plans for the middle part and write their support for their focus. While they are working, walk around the classroom and look for opportunities to provide praise or guidance.

When most students have completed this part of the response, ask again for two or three volunteers to read their leads and middles. Provide a brief time for the class to offer specific positive feedback.

Then make reference to your plan and the note you wrote for your ending, and model how to draft a concise ending that matches this note. It might read something like this:

Since the gift of Sahib was a punishment, Run-Run might have never appreciated the white elephant. But Sahib's persistence fused a lifetime friendship, and he became a permanent part of the lives of Run-Run and Walking Mountain.

Ask the students to refer to their own plans and see what they noted for their endings. Provide time for them to draft. Circulate among them to provide feedback. When they've completed their endings, ask for a few volunteers to share their endings or their entire responses.

Plan and Response

Here is both the plan and the response for a character literature response by Jacob Jenkins. Notice how Jacob used a few words on his plan to remind himself of what he wanted to write.

L

T—Tippy-Toe Chick, Go!

A—George Shannon

Character—Littlest Chick

Trait—Brave

M

stand up to dog

not scared of dog

did more than siblings

E

Thanksgiving, dog chased me

I was brave.

Tippy-Toe Chick, Go! *is a good book. The author of this book is George Shannon. My favorite character is Littlest Chick. Littlest Chick is very brave when he stands up to the dog. Even though Littlest Chick was the smallest, he was a whole lot braver than his mother or his siblings. He was so brave that he stood up to that huge dog. Every time the dog showed up, his mother and siblings ran. But Littlest Chick stood up to that dog. He was so brave and smart. He ran around and around and around the tree and the dog's chain got tangled on the tree. Littlest Chick and his family got to eat their potato bugs. I am the littlest kid in my family, too, and last Thanksgiving we had a cookout. A dog showed up from nowhere. It started barking, and I ran it off. I was brave like Littlest Chick.*

Audience

Give students an opportunity to share their final responses with one another, either with partners or in small groups. Every writer appreciates specific feedback. For additional suggestions on requesting feedback, reread the comments in the introduction (pages 6–7).

GRADING OF A PERSONAL CONNECTION RESPONSE

It is not necessary to grade each response. If you feel a grade is needed, please use a simple rubric and share it with students before they write their responses. Make sure to base your evaluations solely on the listed criteria. Following are two rubrics that you might use for character responses.

Character Response

	Excellent	Satisfactory	Needs Work
Character	Writer identifies one character and a trait that is exhibited throughout the story	Writer identifies one character or a trait	Writer does not identify a character or a trait
Supporting Examples	Writer offers four or more examples of how this trait is exhibited	Writer offers three examples of how this trait is exhibited	Writer offers two or fewer examples of how this trait is exhibited
Vocabulary	Writer uses at least eight specific nouns or verbs in the response	Writer uses 6–7 specific nouns or verbs in the response	Writer uses five or fewer specific nouns or verbs in the response

	Excellent	Satisfactory	Needs Work
Structure	Includes lead, middle, and end	Includes two out of the three main elements	Structure is difficult to identify
Focus	Writing is focused on character and trait	Most of the writing is focused on character and trait	Writing lacks a focus
Voice	Writing has a distinct voice through all or most of the response	Writing has a distinct voice in some of the response	Writing lacks an authentic writer's voice

Lesson Review

1. Discuss character.

2. Create a list of character traits with the students.

3. Create a purpose for writing by discussing why we identify characters and their traits in a story.

4. Read a familiar story with strong characters.

5. Make a list of possible character traits for key characters in the story.

6. Study a sample character response and find key components.

7. Create a simple plan for a lead, middle, and end.

8. Compose a character literature response using the plan as a guide.

9. Invite students to share with an audience and receive specific feedback on what they did well.

Another Look

Reinforcement Lessons for Character Response

Pink and Say

Read the story *Pink and Say* by Patricia Polacco. Ideally, this would be the second or third time that you've read this story to the students. I recommend that you begin a lesson by discussing the three main characters in this story and some traits that fit each one. Place Character Sample 2 (Overhead 5) on the overhead projector. Read it twice to the class. Identify key components of the lead, middle, and end of the response. Provide time for students' prewriting and planning. Finally, ask the students to compose their own character responses for *Pink and Say*.

Akiak

Read *Akiak* by Robert J. Blake to your students, ideally for the second or third time. I recommend that you begin a lesson by noting that Akiak is the only character who the reader actually gets to know. Brainstorm several traits that fit this character in this story. Place the transparency with Character Sample 3 (Overhead 6) on the overhead projector. Read it twice to the class. Identify key components of the lead, middle, and end. Provide time for students' prewriting and planning. Finally, ask the students to compose their own character responses for *Akiak*.

On My Honor

Read *On My Honor* by Marion Dane Bauer. Students need to know this story from a previous reading to be able to listen for character traits. I recommend that you begin a lesson by noting that they need to select either Joel or Tony as a focus for their responses. Brainstorm some possible traits for each boy. Place the transparency with Character Sample 4 on the overhead projector. Read it twice to the class. Identify key components of the lead, middle, and end. Provide time for the students' prewriting and planning. Finally, ask the students to compose their own character responses for *On My Honor*.

Overheads—Character

  The White Elephant

Run-Run is a young elephant trainer in the book *The White Elephant* by Sid Fleischman. Even though this character has very little food and no luxuries in his simple life, he is generous.

Once when bargaining with a beekeeper, he asked for two watermelons.

After his elephant Walking Mountain had watered the road, he gave one watermelon to his elephant and he ate one, even sharing his rind with his massive helper. When Sahib arrived, it put a hardship on Run-Run and Walking Mountain.

Even so, when Walking Mountain acted jealous, Run-Run spoke with his old friend and asked him to accept their visitor gracefully. During his stay with Run-Run and Walking Mountain, there were times that Sahib raided Run-Run's small supply of food. Run-Run never yelled or punished the animal, he simply continued working in the fields to make money to buy more food to feed each of the elephants for the next day. But probably Run-Run's greatest act of selflessness came when the Prince ordered Sahib back to the palace. Before the mahout arrived, Run-Run groomed Sahib, preparing him to go. When Sahib would not kneel so the mahout could mount, it was Run-Run who coaxed the elephant to obey. Even though it broke Run-Run's heart to see the elephant leave, he did not want his new friend to receive a beating. He helped the mahout take Sahib away.

At the end of the story, Run-Run's generosity was rewarded by loyalty.

Sahib returned, and the three friends left to build a life together.

  Pink and Say

In the story *Pink and Say* by Patricia Polacco, Pinkus Aylee rescues an injured Union boy, Sheldon (Say) Curtis, and takes him home to his mother, Moe Moe Bay. This character, who is dedicated to her son, has not left their slave cabin, despite the ravages of the Civil War all around her. She knew that her boy would only know to look for her here. So she waited, hiding from Confederate marauders in her root cellar. Moe Moe Bay tends to Sheldon's injuries as if he were her own son. She consoles Sheldon one night as he admits that he is afraid to return to the war. Even though she prefers that the two boys stay with her, she respects what they need to do. In her final act of dedication, she ushers the boys into the root cellar when they hear Confederate marauders near the cabin. She goes outside to lead them away, and they shoot her. She has given her life for the boys. There is no dedication greater than that of a mother or father. It is a selfless love that knows no limits.

Overheads—Character

OVERHEAD 6 ③ Akiak

Akiak is the name of the protagonist in the book *Akiak* by Robert J. Blake. She is a ten-year-old lead dog for an Iditarod sled team, and this character is determined not only to complete the race, but to win it. As readers, we first see her determination on day three of the race when she and her team take over third place. With 58 teams in the race, this is quite an accomplishment. On day four, they move into second place, but this is when deep snow jams Akiak's pawpad. She couldn't run, and the musher had to remove her from the team. She made arrangements to send Akiak back home. But Akiak wanted to run, so she escaped from the handler, found the trail in a snowstorm and ran to catch up with her team. She followed the scent of her musher and dogs and avoided volunteers who tried to grab her. She found food along the way and drank water from streams where the ice was broken. She never veered from the trail. For six days, she tracked and ran at full speed until she met up with her team. Akiak showed the musher the correct trail to Nome. Even though she couldn't be hooked to the team, she did ride with the winning team into the finish line. Akiak never gave up. She remained determined and triumphed over every obstacle put in her way. She achieved her goal!

OVERHEAD 7 ④ On My Honor

Joel Bates is a conscientious boy who likes to obey his parents and play by the rules. In the book *On My Honor* by Marion Dane Bauer, this character attempts to do what's right, but it isn't enough to save his friend.

Joel tries to talk his best friend Tony out of riding to Starved Rock State Park. He wants to swim at the town pool, but in the end, he gives in to Tony's persistence. Joel tries to talk Tony out of swimming in the Vermillion River. He knows that it is dangerous, but eventually he's lured into the water and enjoys it. When Tony is suddenly missing from sight, Joel dives repeatedly looking for his friend. He even stops a passing car and asks for help. All day long he has fought valiantly to do what he knows is best. It isn't until he gets home after the tragic death of his friend, that Joel cannot do what is right. Keeping his secret tears him apart until he confesses all to Tony's parents and his own.

When Joel follows his conscience and explains what happened at the river, he starts a slow process of forgiving himself and accepting the comfort of others.

38 *Writing Lessons for the Overhead: Responding to Literature* © 2008 Lola M. Schaefer Scholastic Professional

CHAPTER 3

Setting Response

What Is Setting?

Setting is a literary term that sometimes gets lost in the classroom. So much time is dedicated to helping students understand character and plot that discussions of setting often get pushed aside for another day. Some students think of place when they hear the word. Others might associate setting with one particular historical period, like the Civil War. But actually, setting refers to the time, location, and circumstances in which a story takes place.

When studied carefully, setting can be an active tool in developing tone and conflict in a story. For instance, telling scary stories in a well-lit museum during lunch break carries a totally different tone than telling spine-tingling stories in a lantern-lit cemetery on October 31 at midnight. Writers make deliberate choices about setting, and as readers we need to notice the purpose and significance of those decisions.

Think of setting as the nest of the story. The nest provides the best backdrop for the story, bringing layers of meaning that would otherwise be missing. Yes, in a story we need to know when it takes place. Is it spring? Last week? Noon? After the fireworks? The day before the Valentine dance? The morning of the Battle of Gettysburg?

Time is just one consideration. Location is also part of setting. Does the story take place in a backyard? At the Egyptian pyramids? On the top limb of an oak tree? In downtown New York City? Underground, in a mole's tunnel?

Setting can also include circumstances. Sometimes it isn't enough to know that a story takes place in Birmingham, Alabama in 1964. A reader needs to know about the mayor's feelings toward integration, and about what's been happening at the school of the 11-year-old protagonist since the civil rights laws went into effect. Is he treated differently than he was last year? When an author adds these details to the text, the setting is complete. With the time, place, and circumstances laid out clearly, a story can unfold.

Why Teach Setting Response?

We want our students to be critical readers. I can think of no better preparation than helping them examine all of the literary elements used to create compelling stories. Setting is one of these fundamental elements. It can work for the protagonist or against him. Setting can play such a vital role in assisting or obstructing a character's progress that it can almost take on a role, like a character. We want students to take away optimum meaning from what they read. Teaching them the elements of setting will raise their awareness and comprehension of what they read in the future.

We also want students to read like writers. Once they study setting and its influence on a well-written story, they will be better equipped to use it in their own writing. They will know how to put the squeeze on a protagonist by giving her less time to find her sister's antique locket. They will know how to build a rich beach setting so the reader experiences the sand and the sea as a crucial element in their stories. They will see the importance of well-placed details to create an authentic setting for a story.

Introducing Setting

To initiate a discussion on setting, start with these questions for your students, and record their answers on the board or a transparency.

- *What day and month is it?*
- *What time of day is it?*
- *Where are we?*
- *How do you feel? Are you a little tired? Hungry? Anxious to talk to a friend?*

Responses will differ; record three or four, then ask one last question.

- *How would you describe this classroom? Is it drab, colorful, safe, warm, stifling hot, clammy, filled with an energy that could fuel a jet engine? Is it invigorating as a summer storm?*

Students will provide a few descriptions, and you can write the ones you want. Then continue with the lesson.

Teacher: If we were going to set a story here and now, we might select a few of these details to let the reader know when and where the story is going to take place, and what it's like in our classroom. All of this is the setting. The setting of a story tells you where it happens, when it happens, and the circumstances, which means a few details about what it is like at the time of the story. We can remember setting with these terms: Where? When? What is it like?

Let me give you an example. I'm going to describe an opening scene of a story for you. Then you can tell me about the setting.

It was the mid-morning assembly of the five finalists for the spring county-wide spelling bee. Samantha Eggar, a fifth grader, was standing next to sixth grader Elise Capabelli on the stage of the auditorium. Without breaking her smile, Elise whispered into Samantha's ear, "Say you're ill and bow out of this competition right now or your little brother will have an unfortunate accident on the way home from school today."

The smell of Elise's stale breath mixed with the heat of the overhead fluorescent lights and the nervous swell in Samantha's stomach. The room started to spin, and . . .

OK. That's enough for you to answer a few questions. Where does this story begin?

(Students will provide a few examples of what they remember.)
When does this story begin?

(Students will remember that it's at the mid-morning assembly. Someone may remember that it is spring.)
What was it like in the auditorium?

(Student answers will vary.)

What you told me—those details—help create the setting for the beginning of the story. Notice how specific I was. I used terms like *auditorium, mid-morning, spring county-wide spelling bee, stale breath, fluorescent lights, nervous swell.* Writers are always as precise with language as possible to paint pictures in the readers' minds.

Now, let's turn the tables. I'll ask you some questions and you make up some details for the setting of a beginning of a story.

Give me a place, a time, and what it is like for the beginning of a story of two brothers in a kite-flying contest. Think for a moment and make sure your suggestions are specific and paint pictures for the rest of us.

Gives students a few minutes to come up with a story beginning, working alone, in pairs, or in small groups. After several minutes, invite students to share their beginnings.

Student Sample 1

Jackson and Austin stood side by side on top of Hanson's Hill. It was the first day of summer vacation and the city-wide kite-flying contest was to begin in a few moments. These two brothers had a bet riding on the outcome of today's competition, and each boy expected to win. They raised their kites and waited for the starting signal.

Teacher: Let's try that one more time. Give me a place, a time, and what it is like for the beginning of a story of two teens canoeing down a river filled with fallen trees.

Again, allow several minutes for students to work individually or together to create a story beginning.

Student Sample 2

"Left, left!" shouted Suzanne as she paddled furiously.

"I'm doing the best job I can," said Nina, pushing off from yet another log. It was noon on the St. Claire River, and both girls wiped sweat from their foreheads. Neither knew how to steer the canoe, and for the past hour they had spent most of their time freeing their boat from the fallen trees that crisscrossed the water.

Teacher: Excellent work. You know, every story that we read this year will have a setting. Sometimes the place is more important to the story. In other stories, the time will carry more impact. In picture books, the illustrations often give clues to the setting, as well as the words. As we write setting responses, we want to notice how setting can help or hinder the protagonist. It can sometimes add an extra level of conflict. Setting can also create a particular mood for the writing. By studying the importance of setting in our responses, we will learn how to use it more effectively in our own writing. Let's explore setting in a strong story.

THE LESSON—PART 1

Helping Students Identify Setting

We want students to be able to identify the different features of setting in a story. For this lesson, it is important to use a book that is familiar to your students. Since it is easier to introduce and practice literature responses with picture books or short stories, I like to use the book *Granddad's Fishing Buddy* by Mary Quigley.

Before you begin rereading the story, tell the students what you like about it.

Teacher: This is one of my favorite stories because of the setting. When I was a little girl, I used to go fishing with my dad. I loved the quiet of the lake and the glassy look of the water.

All of you need paper and pencil. When you hear anything that describes setting—where, when, and what it's like—write yourself a short note. For instance, if you hear something about the stars looking like night-lights, don't write the whole phrase. Just write *night-lights*. That's enough to help you remember the rest of the image later.

Read the book aloud to the students. Once in a while, repeat a phrase that you think is an especially strong description of the setting. When you've finished, place a blank transparency on the overhead and write three headings: *Where*, *When*, and *What It's Like*. Invite students to share their notes on the setting; they can come up and write their note under the appropriate heading.

Student responses will vary. Here is a list of some images that they might offer.

Where:

- on a lake
- Grandmama and Granddad's cottage on the lake
- in a canoe on a lake
- in the kitchen of the cottage
- a glassy lake
- where the heron stands
- on the pier

When:

- early, early morning
- sky was still blue-black and the stars shone like night-lights
- mid-morning
- bright sky

What It's Like:

- meeting fishing buddy
- can you keep real quiet
- heron stirring up more fish
- can you put a worm on a hook
- out on the lake it was quiet

Teacher: Would anyone like to add anything to these three headings by examining the illustrations?

I've had students offer these details:

- **When:** when the sun makes shadows on the lake

- **Where:** in the lily pads
- **What It's Like:** people waving from their boats

Teacher: Thank you for these great additions. I've placed them on our lists. Now let's circle what you consider to be the two most important entries under each heading. Think about what features help put the reader right inside the most interesting part of the story. Which features have the most influence on the story? Who would like to suggest what is important for the *Where*?

Student responses will vary. Help them understand that two of the most important setting details are places that have to do with the lake and where the heron stands. The story revolves around what takes place on the water. If they say Grandmama and Granddad's cottage on the lake, that's fine. But the kitchen setting is just a segue to the main setting on the lake.

Teacher: Who wants to suggest what is important for the *When*?

Again, keep the students grounded in the main story. They will probably mention morning and mid-morning. If they want to stop after morning, that's fine. It's difficult to determine what season it is, even with help from the illustrations.

Teacher: Who can suggest the two most important details for the *What It's Like*?

Answers will vary, but remind the students that we're looking at the most interesting part of the story. Students of mine have mentioned the quiet of the lake and how the heron stirred up the fish.

Teacher: Thank you for all of your hard thinking. Now, I'd like to show you how to write a literature response that focuses on setting. We're going to think about how setting has an impact on this story.

By now, the students will know what setting is and that it can be important for tone, to increase the conflict, complement the plot, or push the character into action. You can build on this by having them study a literature response that focuses on setting, then plan their own responses. If time permits, proceed into the following lesson.

THE LESSON—PART 2

How Can We Guide Students to Write Their Responses?

If you're picking up the lesson on another day, begin by asking a student to briefly summarize the story of *Granddad's Fishing Buddy*. Then display the lists that students helped you develop for the different details of the setting and review them. As another refresher, ask students to open their writer's notebooks and write a quick explanation of setting, in one or two sentences.

Make sure you provide at least three minutes so students can share with a partner. Then ask the students if anyone heard a great explanation. Ask three or four writers to share with the whole class.

Teacher: I'm glad that you're gaining experience and confidence through our discussions of setting. This year we will be writing quite a few literature responses, and some of those will be focused on setting. I'm going to show you an example of one right now.

Place Setting Sample 1 (Overhead 8) on the overhead projector and read it aloud twice to the students. Draw students' attention to the different components of a well-written literature response focused on setting. If we provide an opportunity for students to discover these components, they are much more likely to include them in their own structured responses. Make sure to include the students as much as possible in the following discussion and identification.

Teacher: Will a volunteer please come to the overhead and underline the title of the book and the author's name? (*after first student is done*) Could another volunteer underline the word *setting* in the lead? (*after second student is done*) Could another volunteer underline the phrase that tells us what the writer says that setting does for this story?

A student should underline "the setting not only offers a backdrop for what happens, but it also establishes tone for the story."

Teacher: Thank you. The setting is the backdrop, or scenery, of the story, and it sets the tone. It is important for us to know how setting contributes to the story. Reread the second paragraph to yourselves. When you complete it, please look up.

Provide a few minutes for the students to reread the second paragraph.

Teacher: Did the writer talk about the backdrop or the tone in this paragraph?

Student: The backdrop.

Teacher: Yes. Now I want you to reread it again and tell me how many examples from the story the writer offered as support.

Some students will say four, referring to the quotes from the text. Some students will say five or six because of the references to the illustrations. And a few will say even more because of the list of terms at the end of the paragraph.

Teacher: Which of these are the most important to you? Which ones give you specific examples of setting?

As students mention specific examples, have them come forward and underline those phrases or words with red marker on the transparency.

Teacher: Please reread the third paragraph again to yourselves. (*after a few moments*) Did the writer talk about backdrop or tone in this paragraph?

Student: The writer discussed tone.

Teacher: Yes, she did. How did the writer describe the tone of this book?

A few students will mention the word *gentle*. Others may say *patient* and *easy*.

Teacher: Could you name some specific examples that the writer provided as support?

As students mention one specific supporting example, invite them to the overhead to underline it in red.

Teacher: Now I'd like you to reread the last paragraph. (*Allow time.*)
What does the writer do in this last paragraph? Is she listing something else that the author did? Does the writer offer a personal connection? Or does the writer make a text-to-text connection?

Student: The writer offered a personal connection to this story.

Teacher: Yes. I agree. That is one way to end any of your literature responses. It isn't necessary, but sometimes a topic or story brings up a memory, and we can add that information at the end of our responses.

If you have time, continue with this lesson. If you need to stop for the day, keep this overhead with students' marks available for the next day's lesson.

Teacher: This is a good, solid literature response that focuses on setting and the impact it has on writing. So a response to setting will include:

- the title of the story
- the author's name
- the word *setting*
- an explanation of the contribution that the setting makes to the story
- specific examples from the story to support this contribution
- an ending

Now, I'd like all of us to plan our own literature response for this story, keeping these ideas in mind. Let's begin by placing an *L* at the top of your paper like this.
This *L* stands for lead. What needs to be in our lead?

Student: The title of the story.

Student: The author's name and the word *setting*.

Student: And what the setting contributes to the story.

Teacher: Let's all add these notes to our leads.

Now, I need to decide what it is that I want to address in my setting literature response. And I'd like you to make that decision, as well. What purpose or use of setting do we want to explain? We can write about the location of the story. We can write about what it was like on the lake that helped make the setting. Or we can write about the time and how that influences the story. I'm going to write about what it was like on the lake. I'm going to show some of the strong images that the author painted with words. I will add that to my plan. Go ahead and write a brief note to yourself about what you're going to say about the importance of the setting in this story. (*Allow time for students to think and make notes on their plans.*)

It is important for all of us to find at least four specific examples to support what we want to write about in our response. Remember, everything has to do with setting. We're not going to summarize the story or talk about character. This is a time to look only at setting and what it does for the story and the reader.

I need to find phrases and terms that help give the reader a sense of the place and time. While I'm looking for my examples, go ahead and think back over the story. If you need to look at the story again, I have a few copies here that you can use. After you've found your examples, return the book to the front of the room so your classmates can use it.

When you're ready, place a large *M* on your plan and write a brief note to yourself about the specific support you want to list in the middle of your response.

Continue with your plan as they work. In my plan, I write several notes. (See sample plan at right.)

Walk through the classroom, reading over shoulders. Nudge those students who seem to be struggling by asking them questions:

- *What part of the setting do you want to write about?*
- *What in the story will support your statement(s) about the setting?*
- *Can you find one description or phrase that supports what you're going to write about?*

When you see student work that is focused and well-supported, make specific comments praising those efforts. Sometimes I stop at this point and have three or four students share their plans with the rest of the class. Even though I have my plan on display, it helps the struggling students to hear what their classmates have chosen to write.

When you feel confident that the students are on the right track and have at least four supporting examples for their thoughts on setting, continue with the plan.

TRANSPARENCY

L

Title—Granddad's Fishing Buddy

Author—Mary Quigley

Setting

What it was like on the lake—how the author took me to the scene and engaged me in the story.

TRANSPARENCY

M

"sending ripples . . ."

"steam lifted from . . ."

" . . . it was quiet . . ."

"ducks and geese flew in . . ."

"fishing lines hung . . ."

"landed near the lily pads."

Teacher: Now it's time to think of an ending. This can be as simple as one sentence that adds another thought to what you've been developing. It can be a personal connection or a text-to-text connection. It can be a general statement about setting and the role it plays in story. Think for a moment about how you would like to end your response. (*While the students are thinking, I add an* E *to my plan.*)

Go ahead and add an *E* to the bottom of your plan.

I've decided to end my piece with a comment on how small details can paint big pictures and have a large impact on the story.

I write *small details—big impression* on the transparency.

Go ahead and write yourself a short note about how you would like to end your literature response.

This is your last time to circulate and offer feedback. Make sure that students have a plan that is usable. After a few minutes, proceed.

Teacher: Is there anyone who would like to share his or her complete plan with the class?

Provide time for a few students to share everything on their plans. Ask the class to tell which of their supporting examples sounds the strongest for what they are writing.

If you have time, proceed in the writing of the literature response. If you need to stop, make sure your students store their plans in a safe place until you can resume.

Guided Writing

You will not have to model every stage of planning a literature response every time, but it is critical that you model the entire process at least once for each of the different literature responses during the year. Students learn so much from watching how we think and plan. As they become comfortable with literature responses—as well as the story elements of character, setting, conflict and theme—they will no longer need your modeling in order to plan a response. You should continue to circulate through the room offering help throughout the year. It is with feedback that you will groom accomplished, focused writers.

Composing the Setting Response

If you are picking up this lesson on a new day, make sure you provide time for each student to read his or her plan to a writing buddy. This helps each student remember what they want to write about, and inspires partners to ask questions of the writer that help him or her go back and improve the plan. Again, students have two choices: They can write the response as one long paragraph, or they can use multiple paragraphs.

Display your plan so all students can see it. Point to the information related to the lead. Then model how to draft a lead for students. It might look something like this:

> In <u>Granddad's Fishing Buddy</u>, the author Mary Quigley uses setting to take the reader to the scene by showing what it was like out on the lake. She paints strong images of the sights and sounds.

Ask students:

- *Do I have the author's name?*
- *Do I have the book's title?*
- *Do I have the word* setting.
- *Do I say what I'm going to write about?*

Teacher: Now take a look at your own plans. Craft a sentence or two that includes the information under your *L* for the lead. You might also try to add a small interesting detail.

Walk around the classroom, asking questions and celebrating any solid or unique leads. When students have completed their leads, give them a moment to reread and revise. Ask for three or four volunteers to share their lead with the class, and provide time for the students to give specific feedback on what the writer did well.

Next, point to your plan and all of the information under the M. Continue using the plan to organize your thoughts and write four to six sentences for the middle. It might look something like this:

> When Sara and her grandfather push off the dock, the author writes, "... sending ripples across the glassy lake." I can see the smooth lake after reading this image. She continues to create a strong setting when she writes, "Steam lifted from the water like clouds." Once they arrive in the middle of the lake, the author gives the reader a sense of calm with, "Way out on the lake it was quiet . . ." She also adds visuals beyond the water with, "... just

---

TEACHER'S COMPLETED PLAN

L

Title—<u>Granddad's Fishing Buddy</u>

Author—Mary Quigley

Setting

What it was like on the lake—how the author took me to the scene and engaged me in the story.

M

"sending ripples ..."

"steam lifted from . . ."

" ...it was quiet ..."

"ducks and geese flew in ..."

"fishing lines hung ..."

"landed near the lily pads."

E

small details—big impression

as the ducks and geese flew in, one by one, boats began to roost . . ." A small detail that any fisherman has witnessed is, "Our fishing lines hung in the water like the tails of fallen kites." To complete the picture, Ms. Quigley offers, "A heron glided over our heads and landed near the lily pads."

Before asking the students to write, give them an opportunity to see how many specific references you noted in your middle. Ask, "Do these examples show ways that the author takes the reader to the lake?" Let's hope they agree that your writing is staying on your focus.

Ask the students to refer to their own plans again and to create a middle for their responses that offers support for their focus on setting. While they are writing their drafts, walk among them looking for opportunities to celebrate good work and help those children who seem to be having difficulty.

When most students have completed this section, you can again ask for volunteers who would like to read their leads and middles. Provide time for the class to give some specific feedback on the specific references that match their focuses.

Then make reference to your plan and the brief note that you wrote for your ending. Model how to draft a short ending that matches this note. It might read something like this:

> By the end of the story, I felt as if I knew the lake. The author's small details, one by one, built a setting that was authentic and created a strong impression for me, the reader.

Ask the students to refer to their own plans and see what they noted for their endings. Provide time for them to draft while you circulate among them. When they pause, ask for a few volunteers to share their endings or their entire responses.

Audience

Feedback from an interested audience is a great motivator for a writer. Always provide time for students to share their responses and request specific comments. This feedback fosters student commitment to future writing. For more suggestions on audience, read the suggestions in the introduction (pages 6–7).

GRADING OF A SETTING RESPONSE

You will not need to grade every response. Learning through reflection is the primary goal. If you feel a grade is needed, use a simple rubric and share it with students so they know what you expect of them.

Setting Response

	Excellent	Satisfactory	Needs Work
Lead	Includes title, author, the word *setting* and importance of setting	Includes three of the four lead elements	Includes fewer than three of the lead elements
Middle	Discusses *where*, *when* or *circumstances* with three or more examples from the text	Discusses *where*, *when* or *circumstances* with two examples from the text	Discusses *where*, *when* or *circumstances* with one or no examples from the text
Focus	Writing is focused on the setting	Most of the writing is focused on the setting	Very little of the writing is focused on the setting

	Excellent	Satisfactory	Needs Work
Structure	Includes lead, middle, and end	Includes two of the three structural elements	Includes one of the three structural elements
Vocabulary	Text includes nine or more specific words or phrases	Text includes 6–8 specific words or phrases	Text includes five or fewer specific words or phrases
Voice	The writing has a distinct writer's voice	Most of the writing has a distinct writer's voice	The writing lacks a distinct writer's voice

Lesson Review

1. Explain that setting can be the Where, When, and What It's Like (circumstances) of the story.
2. Create a purpose for writing by discussing why we want to identify setting in a story.
3. Read a familiar story with a strong setting to the students.
4. Make lists of details from the setting under the headings of *Where*, *When*, and *What It's Like*.
5. Study a sample setting literature response and find key components.
6. Create a simple plan for a lead, middle, and end.
7. Compose a setting literature response, using the plan as a guide.
8. Invite students to share with an audience and receive specific feedback on what they wrote well.

Literature Link

Here is a list of other books that lend themselves to a setting response.

The Blue and the Gray
by Eve Bunting

Hachiko: The True Story of a Loyal Dog
by Pamela S. Turner

Mississippi Bridge
by Mildred Taylor

Mole Music
by David McPhail

On My Honor
by Marion Dane Bauer

Owl Moon
by Jane Yolen

The White Elephant
by Sid Fleischman

Another Look

Reinforcement Lessons for Setting Response

Akiak

Read *Akiak* by Robert J. Blake to students, ideally for the second time. I recommend that you begin a lesson by listing details of the setting under headings of *Where*, *When*, and *What It's Like*. Place the transparency with Setting Sample 2 (Overhead 9) on the overhead projector. Read it twice to the class. Identify key components of the lead, middle, and end of the response. Provide time for students' prewriting and planning. Finally, ask the students to compose their own setting response for *Akiak*.

Yatandou

Read *Yatandou* by Gloria Whelan to students, ideally for the second time. I recommend that you begin a lesson by listing details of the setting under headings of *Where*, *When*, and *What It's Like*. Place the transparency with Setting Sample 3 (Overhead 10) on the overhead projector. Read it twice to the class. Identify key components of the lead, middle, and end of the response. Provide time for students' prewriting and planning. Finally, ask the students to compose their own setting response for *Yatandou*.

Across the Blue Pacific

This book offers an interesting blend of two distinct settings. Students can decide to discuss one or both settings in their responses. Follow the same steps as listed for the books used on samples 2 and 3. Read *Across the Blue Pacific* by Louise Borden and use Setting Sample 4 (Overhead 11) on the overhead projector.

OVERHEAD 8   (1)   ## Granddad's Fishing Buddy

In the book *Granddad's Fishing Buddy* by Mary Quigley, the setting not only offers a backdrop for what happens, but it also establishes tone for the story. The author immediately takes the reader to the location when she talks about Grandmama and Granddad's cottage on the lake. Later when Granddad asks, "Can you keep real quiet . . ." the author begins to create the story's gentle tone.

Most of the story takes place on the lake. The author gives us sensory details about the location with phrases like "ripples across the glassy lake," "steam lifted from the water like clouds," "boats began to roost on the rippled water," and "Way out on the lake it was quiet, except for the smooth sound of fishing line sailing through the air and landing with a plop in the water." The illustrations added to the backdrop with the soft shades of greens and blues and all of the reflections and shadows that he painted in the water. The other terms that added a sense of location were: shore, heron, row, fish, and fishing buddy.

The author weaves a gentle tone with phrases like "out on the lake it was quiet," "Then we always got quiet again, so the fish would come," "He (the heron) stood statue-still," and "We waited for a long time." The writing is patient and easy. Nothing is rushed in this story. Even when Sara catches her fish, the story slows again so they can follow the heron to the opposite shore.

Since I fished often as a young girl with my father, this story captures the setting I remember while sitting in a boat. Not only were we on the lake with the sun rising higher by the hour, but we, too, spoke in hushed tones and waited for the fish.

OVERHEAD 9   (2)   ## Akiak

Setting is a powerful force in the book *Akiak* by Robert J. Blake. The location of the story is the Iditarod Race from Anchorage to Nome, Alaska. The place is accented with "wind, snow and rugged trail." This strong physical setting works as a challenge to Akiak and what she wants to accomplish. The author relies on precise description to keep the reader engaged and worried about the outcome. At one point, Mr. Blake uses this phrase, "Through steep climbs and dangerous descents, icy waters and confusing trails . . ." to heighten the drama. Later, when Akiak is trying to join her team, the author writes, "The wind took away the scent and the snow took away the trail . . ." How can this dog find her team if she can't track? The author uses the setting as an unrelenting antagonist. He says, "She ran and she ran until the blizzard became a whiteout." Even near the end, the team is confused by "a maze of snowmobile tracks." Setting in this book is all about location and circumstances. Combined, they build to create a threat that Akiak will never be able to survive, let alone find her team.

Overheads—Setting

OVERHEAD 10 (3) **Yatandou**

I have never been to a Mali village, but after reading *Yatandou* by Gloria Whelan, I feel as if I have. The location and circumstances of the setting show us how deliberate Yatandou must be to work and find joy in this extreme climate. Both text and illustrations come together to demonstrate the intense heat. The artist's use of a fire-rich palette of oranges, yellows, and reds, creates an almost burning effect in many of the illustrations. He also uses sunlight in the art to show how unrelenting the heat is for these people. Ms. Whelan adds to that when she says, "The heat in the onion fields will burn like a thousand fires." She also describes how Yatandou likes to get out of the sun when she writes, "We pound under the shade of a baobab tree." However, later she explains that even on a walk to find firewood, the sun is still with them, in this sentence, "The hot sun sends our shadows with us." Yatandou lives a simple life, and yet it is made difficult by the desert conditions. As Yatandou explains at the very beginning, "When the hot wind blows from the desert I sleep on our roof." The author and illustrator never let us forget that this heat plays an important role in every aspect of Yatandou's daily life.

OVERHEAD 11 (4) **Across the Blue Pacific**

There are two completely different physical settings in the book *Across the Blue Pacific* by Louise Borden. The main story takes place in a small neighborhood on Orchard Road somewhere in the United States. The story of Ted Walker is set aboard the submarine USS Albacore in the Pacific Ocean. The author weaves these two settings into one poignant story that takes place in 1944–1945 during World War II.

Orchard Road is a safe place where Ted and Molly make snowsailors, Buttons the puppy plays, and people listen to ballgames on the front porch while drinking lemonade. Even at Beechwood School, Molly is able to write letters to her friend Ted in the Pacific, and still concentrate on reading, math, recess, and art. It is because of this caring setting that Molly, Mrs. Walker, family, and friends are able to accept the news that Ted's submarine is lost.

Ted's setting aboard the *USS Albacore* is just the opposite. The circumstances of capturing islands, rescuing downed pilots, finding enemy fleets, keeping their torpedoes ready, and living hundreds of feet below the "cold, dark water" of the Pacific add to the tension and paint a secretive, dangerous world.

The author did a great job of fusing these two settings into a story that is both realistic and hopeful.

CHAPTER 4

Conflict Response

What Is Conflict?

Conflict is the struggle in the plot of a story. It's the reason the reader stays involved in the storyline. The protagonist represents the good, and the antagonist, who thwarts the efforts of the protagonist, is considered bad. The conflict is a result of the author strategically planting positive and negative actions to build the drama in the story.

A conflict is a clash, and it is the clash of protagonist and antagonist, and the clash of positive and negative events, that creates an engaging plot. A character who is involved in a genuine conflict must use any and all resources to triumph. It's through this struggle that the character grows. Conflict is a vital element in literature because it is what grabs a reader and holds his attention. Conflict is at the heart of every story.

Why Teach Conflict Response?

Our students need to be able to recognize the components of conflict. They need to be able to decide if the conflict is external, internal, or a combination of both. When they can identify these elements of conflict in literature, they will be more engaged readers because they will be involved in the action of the story. Students will identify with the characters and the obstacles they face. When students understand conflict, they become more critical readers.

Critical readers anticipate the next scene and watch how that scene escalates the struggle. They notice how the character reacts each time the struggle becomes more difficult. A good indicator of a reader's involvement in a story's conflict is when a student simply "can't put a good book down." It's the plot—the conflict—that is holding his attention. Sometimes readers get so engaged that they try to warn the characters by shouting at them, or they get nervous and bite their nails when they sense more suspense or danger. Comprehension relies on understanding what is happening in the story. An engaged reader is one who can follow the plot, empathize with the character, and predict what might happen next.

Students who can identify conflict in the stories they read include authentic conflict in their own writing. Their stories will reflect a challenge that all people face, and their characters will have opportunities to grow and triumph. This is what we want for children. We want literature to show them examples of how honorable, courageous, or resourceful people face adversity. We want the conflict in a story to show them the best in themselves when they find themselves in difficult situations.

Introducing Conflict

All of us are familiar with conflict, although most students probably aren't aware of it. Sharing just a few of the ways authors create conflict will raise their awareness immediately.

When an author is writing a story, he first decides on what his protagonist needs or wants. Will the dog be able to find his way back to his master? Will the pioneer be able to weather the isolation and physical elements of Montana in 1866 to build the home that she needs and wants?

Once the author decides on what his protagonist wants or needs, then it's time to put obstacles in the way. What will make that dog struggle on his journey? A pack of wild dogs? Inclement weather? A flooding river? Nature might be the antagonist.

What will keep the pioneer from achieving her goal? A greedy neighbor who wants her stake? Will the antagonist frighten the pioneer? Steal her provisions? Run off her livestock? Set her first lean-to on fire?

Once an author has a character/protagonist, a want or need, an antagonist, and possible obstacles, the conflict begins to take shape. Only one more thing is needed. In our lives, we don't just have obstacles; good things happen to us. We achieve something, and then life knocks us down a peg. It's the same in literature. We need to help students discover this for themselves and then have them write short responses that illustrate these points.

Before you ask your students to write a conflict literature response, start with a discussion like this one.

Teacher: If you read a story where only good things happened, do you think you would like it?

Student: Probably not. It would be boring.

Teacher: What if you read a story where every event was bad or sad or frightening?

Student: I stop reading those kinds of books. They're too scary or sad.

Teacher: The best stories have a blend of good and bad events. The clash between the two creates conflict. This conflict is what keeps us reading, turning the page to see what happens next. Conflict is an important part of a strong story.

   Let's talk about a story we all know. Think about the main events in the story, "Little Red Riding Hood." What is the first event in the story that starts the action?

Student: Little Red Riding Hood's mother asks her to take a care package to her grandmother.

Teacher: Is that a good event or bad?

Student: It's nice. It's a good event.

Make this simple graph on the overhead projector or on the whiteboard.

Beneath the graph, write: *1. Mother gives LRRH care package for Granny.*

Teacher: This is a graph that we're going to use to rate the events in this story. The middle line is 0. That means if an event is neither good nor bad, we can graph it

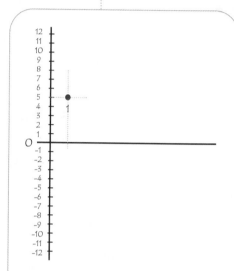

1. Mother gives LRRH care package for Granny.

Making the Graph

❋

I recommend that you do not mass-produce a stack of graphs for conflict graphing. Students can quickly take a sheet of notebook paper and draw the vertical and horizontal axes. The lines on their paper create perfectly spaced notches for the degrees of good or bad comparison.

   For the first time or two, number each of the lines. There's no magic amount for this. I recommend a range of 8–12 degrees of comparison for both the positive and negative events. After the students have graphed a few times and they know what they're doing, it's not necessary for them to number each line. You will notice that on my other examples in this chapter, I do not use numbers on the graph. Children soon realize that the higher dot means better and the lower dot means worse, and that the horizontal axis is neither good nor bad, just neutral.

on that line. If an event is good, we need to decide how good. The higher on the graph, the better the event. The top of the graph is the best—like finding your lost sister or painting an award-winning portrait. The lower on the negative side of the graph, the worse the event. The bottom of the graph is the worst—like losing a pet or being treated unfairly.

We're going to think about each of these events from the reader's point of view—what would be good or bad at that particular time of the story. We're not going to score an event on what we know will happen later, but just at the time it occurs. Let's practice together.

Now, how good is it that Little Red Riding Hood is taking a care package to Grandmother? Is it just barely good, really good, or over-the-top good?

Student: It's not too extraordinary. We could graph it at 4 or 5.

Teacher: Okay. Now, what does her mother tell her not to do?

Students: Talk to strangers.

Teacher: Is this good or bad from the reader's POV?

Point of View in Conflict

❋

A conflict graph is a way of charting a story's main events from the point of view of one character. Writers generally choose the protagonist for this process. It is important that in our modeling we explain how to select one character—whoever it may be—and stay with that one point of view for the evaluation of each event. Conflict needs to be examined from one perspective at a time to be informative, although it is interesting to graph the events in a story from one character's point of view and then from another character's point of view.

Students work in pairs, and together they select the 8–12 critical dramatic events of the story. Each student then takes a different character and makes his or her own conflict graph. Afterward, the students can discuss why their characters perceived each event differently. This works especially well when one student takes the protagonist's POV and the other takes that of the antagonist. For an even greater visual contrast, ask the students to create their conflict graphs on overhead transparencies, each using a different colored marker. At a later time, they can explain their individual choices to the class and then, placing the two graphs on top of one another, show how the same events are weighed differently, depending on the point of view being considered.

Students: Neither really. It's just a piece of advice to keep her safe. It's a little good—like a #1.

Teacher: I'm going to write beneath our graph: *#2 LRRH's mother warns her about speaking to strangers.* Then I'm going to go up to the graph and move a bit to the right of the last dot. I'm putting a second dot on the 0 line and labeling it #2 because it doesn't really have an impact on Little Red Riding Hood at this point in the story.

Teacher Now, Little Red Riding Hood starts through the woods and she meets a wolf. They chat. Is this good or bad at this time for her?

Student: This isn't good, but it's not that bad yet. The dot should go on negative 2 or 3 on the graph.

Teacher: Okay. I'm going to write #3 at the bottom and put: *LRRH meets and speaks with wolf in the woods.* I'm going to move to the right of the last dot and put a dot and #3 on -2. Again, it would seem that a little girl shouldn't speak with a wolf, so I should put a dot in the negative area. However, nothing bad actually happens while they are speaking, so I can't put it much lower than that. Let's continue.

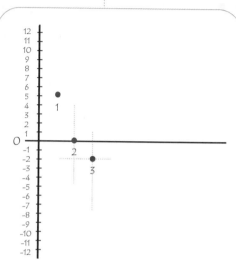

1. Mother gives LRRH care package for Granny.

2. LRRH's mother warns her about speaking to strangers.

3. RRH meets and speaks with wolf in the woods.

Continue this question-and-answer and graphing process with your students for the rest of the story. There are no right or wrong answers as to where to graph each event. Students sometimes disagree when deciding what value to ascribe to an event. This is good. They are engaged in the story and thinking about conflict in a whole new way. To keep the lesson efficient, after minimal discussion, simply ask one student to decide where to put a particular event on the graph, and then move on.

Remind students to make sure they assess each event from the reader's point of view. They also need to evaluate each event as it happens in the story without letting the rest of the story influence their decisions.

These are the story's main events:

1. Mother gives Little Red Riding Hood a care package for Granny.

2. LRRH's mom warns her about speaking to strangers.

3. LRRH meets and speaks with wolf in the woods.

4. Wolf hurries ahead to Granny's house.

5. Wolf tricks Granny and enters her house.

6. Wolf gobbles up Granny.

7. LRRH arrives safely at Granny's house.

8. LRRH is shocked by Granny's new appearance.

9. The Wolf tries to eat LRRH.

10. LRRH runs out and finds a woodcutter.

11. Woodcutter kills wolf and frees Grandmother.

12. Grandmother and LRRH are united.

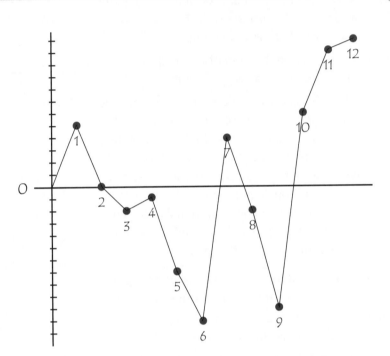

1. Mother gives Little Red Riding Hood a care package for Granny.

2. LRRH's mom warns her about speaking to strangers.

3. LRRH meets and speaks with wolf in the woods.

4. Wolf hurries ahead to Granny's house.

5. Wolf tricks Granny and enters her house.

6. Wolf gobbles up Granny.

7. LRRH arrives safely at Granny's house.

8. LRRH is shocked by Granny's new appearance.

9. The Wolf tries to eat LRRH.

10. LRRH runs out and finds a woodcutter.

11. Woodcutter kills wolf and frees Grandmother.

12. Grandmother and LRRH are united.

Teacher: Now let's connect the dots, starting with the first event and ending with the last, in the order that we wrote them.

I start to connect the dots until our graph looks like the one on page 60.

Teacher: Did this story have all good events in it?

Student: No.

Teacher: Did this story have only bad events in it?

Student: No. It had both good and bad.

Teacher: What do you notice about the good and bad events?

Student: They are mixed up in the story.

Student: Some are a little good, a lot good, or a little bad or very bad.

Student: But at the end of the story the events are pretty good.

Teacher: This up-and-down motion that we see on our graph is conflict that was produced by putting these events together in this order. There are a few really dramatic events, like when the wolf eats Granny and when the woodcutter kills the wolf. Notice that the worst events take place near the end of the story. This conflict builds and builds until the climax—the highest point of dramatic tension. When the woodcutter kills the wolf and removes Granny, we know that everything will be OK. The wolf is now gone and Granny and Little Red Riding Hood are now safe.

This is a good stopping point for your initial discussion of conflict. If you have additional time and sense your students' involvement and enthusiasm, continue with the next part.

Conflict Graphing

I wish I could say that I invented conflict graphing, but actually I initially saw it described years ago in a book called *Literacy Through Literature* by Terry D. Johnson and Daphne R. Louis (1987). I have used this graphing technique over the years, and students always enjoy it. One year, two third grades in our elementary school created class-size graphs of the events in *Hatchet* by Gary Paulsen, and posted them in the hall on the same day. The conversations that arose as students adamantly argued the placement of events were something to hear.

Conflict graphing that prepares children to write a conflict literature response provides a visual of how many dramatic scenes are in a story. I usually suggest to students that they select the 8–12 most important events to graph. I also remind them that each event needs to be evaluated from the point of view of one character—usually the protagonist.

Purpose of the Conflict Graph

❋

Conflict graphing inspires students to think more deeply about what events actually make up the conflict of a story and teaches them to think critically about how each of those events affects the overall story. I've asked students to write conflict responses with and without the graph work. Responses written after the graphing exercise are always much more thorough and thoughtful. This is not to say students need to graph conflict every time they write a conflict response. Once students know the process of studying conflict, they will go through the story and find the dramatic turning points. You will see evidence of this in their responses.

THE LESSON—PART 1

How Can We Help Students Identify Conflict?

Listing the key dramatic events in the story enables students to look at the graph quickly and see which negative events spurred the protagonist into action. Some stories start with a bang, like someone falling into a ravine, or a boat sinking. This immediate drama forces the protagonist to take action. Other stories start out gently, and after a while, an event takes place that changes the course of the story. Still others build gradually to one climactic scene near the end of the story.

One thing we would like students to recognize while graphing conflict is that almost every book written for young people ends on a hopeful note. That doesn't mean "happily ever after," just hopeful. In other words, all ending actions are plotted on the positive axis. Most stories begin on the positive axis, as well. These are patterns that students typically only notice when they dig in and study each of the main dramatic events with scrutiny. A reader is usually so captivated by the storyline, that he or she does not notice how the author crafted the plot. But during graphing, they do.

I try to always model new experiences with well-known stories. Since you have already introduced graphing with "Little Red Riding Hood," I would suggest that you continue this lesson by reading a traditional version of this story aloud to your students.

Teacher: I'm going to read "Little Red Riding Hood" aloud to refresh all of our memories. As I'm reading the story, I'd like you to sit with a pencil and paper and jot down what you consider to be the story's two key dramatic events. Don't write much, just a word or two.

For instance, when the wolf tries to eat Little Red Riding Hood, you could simply write *wolf eats LRRH* in your notes.

After you read the story aloud to your class, put the conflict graph that you composed in a highly visible place.

Teacher: Let's first review the dramatic events that we graphed.

Read through each of the events at the bottom of the graph.

Teacher: Did anyone write a note for a key dramatic event that is not listed on our graph? Is there anything we need to add?

Depending on the version of the story that you read, one or two students may have additions, or slight revisions of the scenes. If students do make suggestions, make sure to thank them for their careful listening.

Teacher: Let's take a good look at where the story starts. Does it start with a good or bad event? Remember, we are evaluating these events from the reader's point of view.

Student: It begins with a good event.

Teacher: Many stories do begin that way. What is the first event that is plotted on the negative half?

Student: The scene where Little Red Riding Hood meets and speaks with the wolf.

Continue with this kind of questioning as you zero in on the worst event and the event where the situation starts to improve to the best event.

Teacher: Does this story end with a good or bad event?

Student: It ends with a good event.

Teacher: It does. In fact, most if not all of the stories that we read this year will end with a positive event. All fairy tales and traditional tales tend to have over-the-top happy endings.

You will see a pattern this year that stories try to offer hope or the idea that in the end, things will be better. An author wants to satisfy the reader and end the story on a positive note.

I have another question for you. Do most of the events happen around Little Red Riding Hood, or are they things she thinks and worries about?

Student: Most of the actions are things that happen outside or around her.

Teacher: I agree. This kind of conflict, where the protagonist or main character reacts to what is happening, is called external conflict. In other words, things happen that cause the protagonist to act in a certain way.

But sometimes there are stories where the protagonist is struggling more on the inside. Maybe he or she has a difficult decision to make, or the main character is dealing with an issue:

fear, humiliation, worry, or some other powerful feeling. In this kind of conflict, there is usually something external that triggers the internal conflict of the protagonist. Most stories are a blend of both.

I have another question. Would you say the events in this story create mild conflict or extreme conflict?

Student: Some events aren't all that dramatic, but some are, like when the wolf eats the grandmother.

Teacher: An easy way to judge this is to look at your graph. Are there places where the plotting of the lines goes down far on the graph, then high on the graph? Those are places where the conflict is extreme. If there are only small dips and rises, then the conflict is mild.

Student: I think the conflict is extreme because you have an animal eating a person and then that animal getting killed. That's dramatic.

Teacher: Yes it is. For such a short story the conflict is quite extreme. Could you list for me the most dramatic scenes in the story?

Students may list:

- Wolf gobbles up Granny.
- Wolf tries to eat Little Red Riding Hood
- Woodcutter kills wolf and frees Granny
- Granny and Little Red Riding Hood are united

(If students select other scenes, have them provide reasons why they are dramatic. Then go back and look at the graph. Any dramatic scene should exceed at least the #5 on the graph.)

In this part of the lesson, we read the entire story aloud and discussed how the story began and ended. We studied where many events were graphed. We explored the concept of external vs. internal conflict and noted that the conflict in this particular story was extreme, or dramatic. This is a natural stopping place.

THE LESSON-PART 2

How Can We Guide Students to Write Their Responses?

If you're picking up the lesson on another day, briefly review the conflict graph and ask students to write a brief definition of conflict. Have a volunteer or two share to make sure everyone understands the concept. Now, it's time to examine a sample conflict response.

Teacher: I'm very pleased at the way all of you have participated in our graphing and discussions of conflict. Now I'd like to show you a sample conflict response for "Little Red Riding Hood."

Put Conflict Sample 1 (Overhead 12) for "Little Red Riding Hood" on the overhead projector and read it aloud twice.

Teacher: Will a volunteer please come to the overhead and underline the title of the story and the word *conflict*? (*Allow time for a student to underline these in the lead.*)

Who can tell me how the author describes the conflict in that first sentence?

Student: The writer says the conflict begins gently.

Teacher: Begins gently. Yes. Could you please come up here and underline those words in blue, as well? Thank you.

Who can find the next time that the word *conflict* appears in this response?

Student: I see it again in the seventh line.

Teacher: How does the writer describe the conflict here?

Student: He says that the conflict of the story escalates.

Teacher: What does the word *escalate* mean?

Student: It's more than before.

Student: It grows.

Teacher: (*asking one student*) Would you come up here and underline that phrase in blue? Thank you. And, again, do you see the word *conflict* anywhere else in this response?

Students will identify and underline the word *conflict* three more times in this response and explain what the author is saying about conflict at those times.

Teacher: Now, I'd like us to look for support. What I mean is that I want us to look for specific references to the story that prove what the writer is saying in this response. Let's start back at the beginning where he mentions that the conflict begins gently. In a literature response, a writer has to show specific events from the story that prove the beginning conflict was gentle. What specific events does this writer use to make his point?

Student: Mother gives Little Red Riding Hood a basket of food for her grandmother.

Student: Mother warns her daughter to beware of strangers in the woods and cautions her not to speak to them.

Student: Little Red Riding Hood meets a wolf and he hurries ahead of her to Granny's.

Teacher: Excellent support. This writer uses four different examples right from the story. Why do you think he called these examples of gentle conflict?

Student: Because they're not really bad or really good. They're just in that middle zone on the graph.

Teacher:	I agree with you. Now, let's look at the next time the author mentions conflict. (*Point to the middle of the first paragraph.*) What happened in the story to make this writer say that the conflict escalated?
Student:	The wolf gobbled up Granny.
Teacher:	Yes. And did the writer mention any other dramatic scene?
Student:	Yes. When the wolf tries to eat Little Red Riding Hood.
Teacher:	Excellent. You all are critical readers today. I appreciate it. Look ahead to the part here where the writer mentions internal conflict. What is his proof for mentioning that in the response?
Student:	When Little Red Riding Hood notices how different Granny looks.
Teacher:	Any other proof?
Student:	When she realizes what the wolf did to Granny.
Teacher:	Exactly. The writer offered two examples of internal conflict. Now, here at the very end, what one example does the writer mention to show that the story went back to external conflict?
Student:	When the woodcutter saves the day.
Teacher:	This is a well-written conflict response. What makes it so good is that the writer gives us plenty of events from the story to prove what he is saying about the conflict. I hope that as we plan and write our conflict responses, all of you refer back to our conflict graph and use specific examples from the story to prove your point.

I'd also like you to make a list of these words. You won't use all of them each time you write a response, but you will use many of them when you explain the conflict in a story. |

- conflict
- external/internal
- dramatic
- mild/gentle
- climactic scene
- beginning
- ending
- protagonist/main character

Let's begin to plan our own conflict responses to this story by putting an *L* at the top of our papers. Let's list the title of the story. This is a traditional tale, so there is no author. And let's add the word *conflict* to the plan for the lead. (*Allow time to do this.*)

Next to the word *conflict*, add a word to indicate what you want to say about the conflict in this story. This doesn't have to have proof yet, but I do want you to say something about how dramatic or mild the conflict is for most of the story. I'm going to add the word *dramatic* to my plan. (*Allow time for thinking and adding the one-word note.*)

Next, on your plan add an *M* for the middle of your response. For the middle, we want to talk about one aspect of the conflict. You can choose from these:

- external
- internal
- beginning of the story
- ending of the story

Take a moment to think about what you would like to discuss in your response.

Pause for a few minutes to give students time to think.

Teacher: Now, write down which aspect you chose, making sure you can support it with three or four examples from the story. Let's go ahead and add the word *support* beneath our choices.

I'm going to select the ending of the story for my plan.

Now, let's add a word or two right now so we know which events will offer us support for our middle statement. For instance, for my middle, I'm going to be talking about the extremely dramatic events at the end of the story, so I'm going to write some notes to myself.

I'll wait a few moments while you decide what proof from the story will support your statement in the middle. Don't forget to look up and refer to the conflict graph. I also have a few copies of the story. You can also come up and look over the story again for a few minutes.

Provide a few minutes for this type of planning. Circulate around the room and ask questions of those children who haven't made their decisions. Rather than telling them what to write, give them choices of topics. Once they've selected a topic, ask them what events they will use as proof for the points they want to make.

Meanwhile, celebrate sound examples that support the writer's statement. It's the celebration that has the most carryover effect. You can even stop occasionally and ask a student to share what's on his or her plan. Sometimes just hearing another student's ideas can provide the spark of inspiration for a student who is stalled.

Teacher: When you have all of your notes for the middle section of your response, look up so I know you're ready to continue.

We are now ready for the ending of the response. Go ahead and add an *E* to your plan. For the ending, you have several choices. You can write a sentence or two about how this conflict engaged you in the story and made you want to read on, or you can discuss why you were not engaged.

You can also explain the general pattern of conflict for the whole story—how it began and how it ended, or you could

L

Title—Little Red
        Riding Hood

Conflict

M

the ending of the story—
extreme conflict

Support

M

the ending of the story—
extreme conflict

support—
        W gobbles Granny

        W tries LRRH

        WoodC kills W

        Granny is free

Sharing Plans

While you are helping students develop brief plans for their responses, stop often, at different stages, and ask for volunteers to share what they have on their plans. You only need two or three students to share each time. Even if they only have a few notes, this sharing accomplishes three things.

- It is another way to keep students engaged in the process and their energy focused.

- Sharing helps students who are struggling with their plans. Hearing what other students have written triggers ideas in them.

- It provides a quick assessment, so you know what you've explained well and what might need additional work.

TRANSPARENCY

E

killing as solution to a problem

conflict in tall tales vs. current contemporary literature

write a comment or two about how you plan your conflict in the stories that you write. You may also have a completely different way that you want to end this response. No matter what you select, you will need to use the word *conflict* again somewhere in your ending.

I'm going to add notes to my plan. (*See sample shown at left.*) My plan is now complete. I will give you a few moments to plan the ending for your responses. Remember to include the word *conflict* somewhere in your ending.

Circulate around the room and celebrate original endings that add meaning to the response. Offer assistance to students who are struggling by asking questions.

You can help students write their responses, or you can stop here and resume with the writing on another day.

THE LESSON-PART 3

Composing the Conflict Response

The sample response was relatively brief. Let the students know that you are not interested in long responses, but in well-written ones with specific examples from the story used as support. If this is one of the first times that your students have written a literature response, you will want to model how to begin. First review the information on your plan for your lead. Then model drafting a lead for students. It might look something like this:

In the story "Little Red Riding Hood" the conflict starts out mild, but soon becomes quite dramatic when the reader learns of Wolf's true intentions.

Now, point to your lead and ask the students:

- *Do I have the title of the story?*
- *Do I have the word* conflict *in my lead?*

Teacher: Now look at your own plans and craft a one- or two-sentence lead that will pull the reader into your response. Make sure to include all of the information on your plan for the lead, plus a little zip that will intrigue your reader.

Walk around the classroom peeking over shoulders and pointing out leads that are solid or unique. Then ask for volunteers to read. This is a time for the other students to talk about what the writer did well. It's not time for criticism. That kind of feedback at this early stage would only turn off the writer. After listening to three or four leads, provide three to four minutes for everyone to reread and possibly revise their own leads.

Continue to refer to your plan as you organize your thoughts, then write four to five sentences for the middle. The middle of your response might look something like this:

As soon as Wolf gobbles up Granny, the reader is engaged, worried for Little Red Riding Hood's safety. The tension continues to build when Little Red Riding Hood arrives. From that scene forward, the conflict is quite dramatic until it climaxes near the end of the story when Wolf tries to eat Little Red Riding Hood. Shocked and frightened, Little Red Riding Hood runs out of Granny's home and finds a woodcutter, who returns with her. In an extremely dramatic scene, the woodcutter kills Wolf and cuts him open. Granny is alive. All is well.

Circulate through the classroom calling attention to students who have followed their plans and supported their ideas with specific references to the story. Ask questions to support the students who are struggling. Refer these children back to their plans, suggesting that they write what they have already decided upon.

Once students start completing their middles, I ask for a few volunteers to read theirs aloud. Again, students should only give positive feedback at this point.

Next, refer back to your plan and read your notes for the ending aloud.

**TEACHER'S
COMPLETED PLAN**

L

Title—Little Red
       Riding Hood

Conflict

M

the ending of the story—
extreme conflict

support—
    W gobbles Granny
    W tries LRRH
    WoodC kills W
    Granny is free

E

killing as solution to
a problem

conflict in tall tales vs.
current contemporary
literature

Take a moment to mentally craft your ending. It might look something like this:

> Wolves gobbling up people. Woodcutters opening up wolves. Traditional tales use graphic methods to build and resolve conflict. Today's picture books rely on less violent resolutions.

Ask the students to reread their plans for their endings, think about what they want their endings to say, and then write endings for their responses. Remind students to make their final point as specific as possible. Encourage them to use an example from the text to help them make a point in their ending. As they work, walk around the room and mention what individual students are doing well. When most students have crafted an ending, ask for a few volunteers to share their ending, or all of their response, for positive feedback.

Student Conflict Response

❋

This is a conflict response written by fourth grader Katherine Keys on *Rudi's Pond* by Eve Bunting.

> *Rudi's Pond by Eve Bunting shows dramatic conflict. It shows emotion that drags you in and through the book, from Rudi and the narrator having fun together to when Rudi goes to the hospital. His classmates think he is going to get better. They make him a get well sign, but the narrator finds out that Rudi has died. Follow the emotion and happiness. You will cry and smile.*
>
> *The conflict in this story had an impact on me because my great-grandmother died. It touched all of my family's lives.*

Katherine's emotions were stirred by the conflict in this book. She mentioned a few key events that showed the happiness and sadness of the story. At the end of her response, Katherine wrote about why this book was relevant to her. Even though this piece is brief, it addresses every point needed for a conflict response. This student feels successful, as she should, and will be eager to write another literature response in the future.

GRADING OF A CONFLICT RESPONSE

There is no need to grade every literature response. When you do need formal evaluation, read the suggestions on the use of rubrics in Chapter One (page 19). The following rubrics can be used as examples for creating your own.

Audience

~~~~~~~~~~~~~~~~~~~~~~~~~

For a review of the importance of audience, see the introduction (pages 6–7). Always provide some time for students to receive targeted feedback. It fuels their writing in the future.

Conflict Response

	Excellent	Satisfactory	Needs Work
Lead	Includes title, author, the word *conflict*, and description of conflict	Includes three of the four lead criteria	Includes two or fewer of the lead criteria
Conflict Graph	Graph is legible and has ten or more graphed events	Graph contains 6–9 graphed events	Graph is difficult to read and has five or fewer graphed events
Focus	Writing is focused on the described conflict	Some of the writing is focused on the described conflict	Little or none of the writing is focused on the described conflict

	Excellent	Satisfactory	Needs Work
Structure	Includes lead, middle, and end	Includes two of the three structural elements	Structure is difficult to identify
Supporting Examples	Response includes at least four specific examples from the text	Response includes three specific examples from the text	Response includes fewer than three specific examples from the text
Voice	Writing has a distinct voice through all or most of the response	Writing has a distinct voice in some of the response	Response lacks an authentic writer's voice

Lesson Review

1. Explain that conflict is the result of positive and negative events in a story.
2. Create purpose for writing by discussing why we want to identify conflict.
3. Reread a familiar story to students.
4. Select a specific point of view from which to study the events of the story, e.g., the protagonist, the antagonist, the narrator, or the reader.
5. Create a conflict graph to select key dramatic events of a story.
6. Review the graph and discuss mild or dramatic conflict.
7. Explain the difference between internal and external conflict.
8. Study a sample conflict literature response and find key components.
9. Create a simple plan for a lead, middle and end.
10. Compose the literature response using the plan as a guide.
11. Have students share with an audience and receive feedback on what they did well.

Another Look

Literature Link

Here is a list of other books and stories that lend themselves to a conflict response.

Across the Blue Pacific
by Louise Borden

Freedom Summer
by Deborah Wiles

The Memory String
by Eve Bunting

*Simply Sarah:
Anyone Can Eat Squid*
by Phyllis
Reynolds Naylor

Sitting Bull Remembers
by Ann Turner

Swift
by Robert J. Blake

The White Elephant
by Sid Fleischman

Reinforcement Lessons for Conflict in Story

Akiak

Read *Akiak* by Robert J. Blake, ideally for the second time. Begin a lesson on conflict graphing, perhaps identifying the first two critical events of the story. Encourage students to consider each scene from Akiak's point of view, and then have each student complete his or her own graph. Provide time for student partners to compare graphs and discuss their choices. (See page 73 for a sample conflict graph for *Akiak*.)

Place the transparency with Conflict Sample 2 (Overhead 13) on the overhead projector. Read it twice to the class, identifying key components. These include:

- what is included in the lead sentence
- how the writer talks about conflict in the middle
- specific events from the story that the writer uses to support his or her statements
- how the writer ends the response

Provide time for students' prewriting where they plan what they want to write, using their graphs as a tool to think about the conflict in the story. Finally, ask the students to compose their own conflict response for *Akiak*.

Provide an opportunity for students to share their responses with an audience and receive feedback on what they did well.

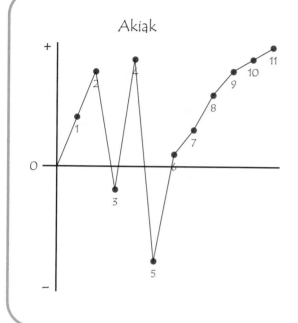

Akiak

1. The Iditarod Race begins.
2. Akiak leads her dog team, never getting lost.
3. Willy Ketchum teases that Akiak is too old to make it.
4. Akiak leads her team to take over first place.
5. Deep snow jams Akiak's pawpad and she is removed from the team.
6. Akiak escapes before she is flown home.
7. Akiak avoids volunteers and runs after her team on the trail.
8. Akiak finds water and discarded food to nourish herself.
9. Akiak runs and catches up to her team.
10. The dog finds the correct trail for her team.
11. Akiak rides on the sled to the finish line and is welcomed into Nome.

On My Honor

On My Honor by Marion Dane Bauer is a 90-page novel that you can read to your students over the course of a few days. If you have a class set, each student can read two chapters a day. This story is a wonderful example of internal conflict. Even though Joel's predicament and sorrow result from external events, the main conflict is the internal process of how he deals with the death of his friend.

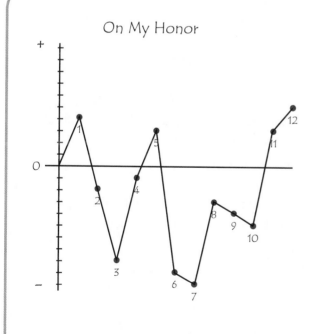

On My Honor

1. Joel and Tony head out on their bikes to the Starved Rock State Park.
2. Tony stops on the bridge and the two boys go swimming in the Vermilion River.
3. Tony disappears from sight as the two boys swim out to a sandbar.
4. Joel dives into muddy waters, searching for Tony.
5. Joel asks a young man to help him search for his friend.
6. Joel accepts that his friend has drowned.
7. Joel blames his dare for the cause of Tony's death.
8. Joel decides to hide in his room from the truth.
9. At first, Joel does not tell the truth to his family or Tony's parents.
10. Joel struggles with hiding the truth and fibbing about what he knows.
11. Joel tells all to his family, Tony's parents, and the police.
12. Joel's father comforts him.

Follow the same steps outlined in the first two lessons. Students will want to view the conflict from Joel's point of view. To keep them from selecting too many events and feeling overwhelmed, you might suggest that your students select one key event from each of the 12 chapters as they read through the book. If you read the book to the students, you might decide to create one large conflict graph instead of individual graphs. (See sample graph, page 73.)

Place Conflict Sample 3 (Overhead 14) on the overhead projector and read it to the class twice. Review the structural elements with students. Continue the process through planning, writing the response, and sharing.

When Marian Sang

When Marian Sang by Pam Muñoz Ryan is a picture book biography. It is a compelling story, but it is also a work of narrative nonfiction. Begin as you did with the first three conflict lessons.

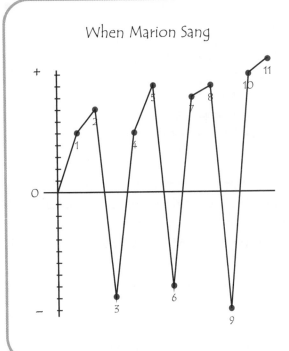

When Marion Sang

1. Marian enjoys singing as a child.
2. Marian performs with choirs in Philadelphia.
3. At eighteen, a music school denies admittance to Marian because of her race.
4. A performance at the Metropolitan Opera inspires Marian to pursue her dream.
5. Marian performs around the US to enthusiastic audiences.
6. She cannot travel or stay in hotels with Caucasians.
7. Marian studies with Giuseppe Boghetti.
8. She studies in Europe and then performs for many appreciative audiences.
9. Marian returns to the US and Constitution Hall will not let her perform because of her race.
10. Marian sings at the Lincoln Memorial to 75,000 people.
11. Marian has a wonderful singing career that is topped with a performance at the Metropolitan Opera.

After you have developed and studied a conflict graph (see sample, above), place the transparency with Conflict Sample 4 (Overhead 15) on the overhead projector.

Follow the same steps as in Lessons 1, 2, and 3.

Overheads—Conflict

  ## Little Red Riding Hood

In the traditional tale of "Little Red Riding Hood," the conflict begins gently with some everyday events. Mother gives Little Red Riding Hood a basket of food to take to her Granny. Mother also warns her daughter to beware of strangers in the woods and cautions her not to speak to them. Even when Little Red Riding Hood meets a wolf and he hurries ahead of her to Granny's house, nothing really bad has happened in the story. But when the wolf gobbles up Granny, the conflict of the story escalates. The story reaches its dramatic climax when the wolf tries to eat Little Red Riding Hood. She is now faced with the greatest struggle of the story. As with all traditional tales, the ending offers Little Red Riding Hood and the reader safety and security. The woodcutter kills the wolf. And even though death is usually a bad thing, in this story it's good for Little Red Riding Hood because this action frees Granny. The story leaves the reader satisfied that Granny and Little Red Riding Hood will now be together and happy.

For the most part, this story's tension is created through external conflict. In other words, most of the action happens outside Little Red Riding Hood. There is some internal conflict when she notices that Granny looks different than usual. It intensifies when the wolf tries to eat her and she realizes what has happened to Granny. But the story quickly reverts back to external conflict when the woodcutter saves the day.

  ## Akiak

One critical event in the book *Akiak* by Robert J. Blake defines the dog's struggle and the story's conflict. At the beginning of the story Akiak is the lead for a dog team that is running the Iditarod Race. She is excited. She is driven. She is strong and never gets her team lost. She even leads her team into second place. At this point of the story, there really doesn't seem to be any conflict. Everything is going well. But then, deep snow jams her pawpad and she cannot run. Akiak is removed from the team and prepared to be taken home. Akiak escapes as she is being loaded onto an airplane. From there she survives on her own. The dog finds the trail again, eludes volunteers who try to capture her, and nourishes herself with water and discarded food along the way. She runs, all by herself, on and on, over ice and snow until she meets up with her team. Her determination wins out over all of the obstacles that have been in her way. This is a story with external conflict and about how one dog rises above it all to join her master and ride on the dog sled to the end of the race in Nome, Alaska. Even though this conflict did not have the usual back and forth between good and bad events, it was compelling. As a reader, I kept turning the pages to see if the dog would make it. And she did!

3 # On My Honor

The conflict in the book *On My Honor* by Marion Dane Bauer is mostly internal. Joel doesn't even want to go to Starved Rock State Park at the beginning of the story, but because his dad gives him permission and his best friend Tony urges him to go, he does. Every dramatic scene is about Joel's inner struggle with the events of that day. When Tony stops on a bridge over the Vermillion River, Joel becomes uncomfortable and reminds Tony that they said they were going to the State Park. When Tony goes into the river, Joel hesitates, then eventually follows, but is not enthused about the idea. However, once in the river and swimming vigorously, Joel starts having fun until . . . he cannot see Tony. The conflict intensifies at that moment. Now Joel has to decide if his friend is playing a trick on him or in serious trouble. Joel does dive and search for his friend in the murky waters. He stops a young man in a car and has him search, too. Ashamed and guilty, Joel goes home but doesn't tell anyone what has happened. He becomes angry as his feeling of guilt escalates. This is a story where most of the events are negative and a source of turmoil for Joel. The conflict is never really resolved, however the ending is hopeful.

4 # When Marian Sang

The conflict in the book *When Marian Sang* by Pam Muñoz Ryan is created by these two facts: Marian Anderson had great musical talent and she was treated unfairly in the United States because of racial bias. Marian's talent was recognized at an early age, and she began to sing with choirs. When she and her family wanted her to receive musical training, the school would not accept her because of the color of her skin. Later, she toured several cities in the United States. The crowds received her enthusiastically in the concert halls, but quite often she was not allowed to ride with Caucasians on the train, or sleep in certain hotels because of her skin color. Marian rose above this adversity and pursued her dream of singing for many people around the world. She traveled to Europe to study voice, and later she entertained audiences all over that continent. But when she returned to the United States, she was not allowed to sing at Constitution Hall. Public outcry was so strong that a concert was scheduled at the Lincoln Memorial, and finally she sang, for 75,000 people. Her struggle was created by external obstacles beyond her control. The conflict in this biography is extreme because every time Marian's career started to take off, racism restricted her. Her triumph at the end of the story was when she sang at the Metropolitan Opera—a lifelong dream.

CHAPTER 5

Theme Response

What Is Theme?

Many students are familiar with the word *theme*, but that doesn't guarantee they know exactly what it means. It is not the message of the book, the plot, a summary, a moral, or the reason the author wrote the story. Theme is a universal truth that is shown or exemplified through the telling of a story. A universal truth is a statement that can be true for anyone, anytime, anywhere.

One good deed deserves another is a truth that is accepted by most people everywhere. Not all universal truths are stated as proverbs or adages, but many of them take the form of maxims because they have been accepted by people for a long time, and many have been recorded in such forms around the world. A truth is usually stated in positive terms and can be the original work of the writer. In fact, students who rarely know many proverbs or adages do a wonderful job of stating a theme in their own words.

Why Teach Theme Response?

Stories are written to entertain and share human experiences. As readers, we relate to well-defined characters and their plights. We connect with the protagonists emotionally and hope for their successes or survival. We cheer for these characters and discover what resources, both intellectual and emotional, we possess. When good overcomes evil, or the resourceful protagonist achieves a goal, we celebrate. It's only natural that we also relate to the beliefs that define these characters. Each time we revisit a powerful, well-written story, it offers us hope. We agree. We laugh. We cry or worry. But in the end, there's hope. If we see these themes as truths that sustain our literary heroes, it affirms their importance for us.

Introducing Theme

How does an author decide on a theme? I can't speak for all authors, but many writers don't consciously plant a theme in a story. Instead, themes appear in our works because our beliefs about people and life are always a part of anything we write. Authors typically aren't even aware of the themes of their stories until they have had an opportunity to go back and revisit their words.

Stories have multiple themes, and every reader experiences a story's themes in an individual way, based on his or her past experiences and beliefs. One reader might recognize the theme as *Courage is the first step toward freedom*, while another person might read the same story and identify the theme as *The need for freedom spurs us to find hidden strengths*.

Here is a quick way to prepare students before you ask them to write a theme literature response.

Ask your students if they are familiar with the story "The Three Little Pigs." If most are, then proceed. If not, find a familiar tale that most of your students do know.

Teacher: Many stories have multiple themes. Let's see if "The Three Little Pigs" is one of them. For instance, can anyone think of a universal truth—keep it short—using the word *teamwork* or *team*? I could say *Work goes quicker with teamwork*. Now you try.

Students may respond with:

- *Teamwork pays off.*
- *It's easier to fight off an enemy when you work as a team.*
- *Teamwork brings out the best in everyone.*

Teacher: Great themes. And I like that they are all different. Let's try that again. Create a theme for "The Three Little Pigs" using the word *prepare* or *preparation*. For instance, *Preparation wards off worry*.

Students may respond with:

- *Be prepared.*
- *Preparation can prevent disaster.*
- *Prepare for the worst and be surprised by the best.*
- *Preparation beats a lot of huffing and puffing.*

Teacher: Are some themes wrong and others right?

Student: Some themes work better for the story.

Student: No theme is wrong, but some are stronger.

Teacher: I agree. There are no right or wrong themes. Each reader might select a different theme or phrase the same thought differently. People's original themes reflect their experiences and how the story resonates with them. Each person discovers an underlying truth that he or she believes, and the story brings that to the surface.

We are going to write theme literature responses this year so we can think about underlying themes. In our responses, we will select our very own themes—truths that are important to us and that the story proves. By writing these responses, we will see the connection between character and conflict and theme. What the protagonist does and says in his struggle illustrates the theme.

It's possible that some stories don't have a theme, but I think it's safe to say that all excellent literature—stories with strong protagonists who are forced to rely on their own resources to survive or succeed—contains themes. In these kinds of stories, there are usually turning points where the character makes decisions and acts on those decisions. In scenes like these, theme seems to rise to the surface.

THE LESSON–PART 1

How Can We Help Students Identify Theme?

We want students to be able to find the truth in a story that is meaningful to them, and we want students to support the themes they choose with details or events directly from the story.

To help them reach these goals, we can start by choosing a familiar story. Before you reread the story, tell the children that you would like them to jot down any "important" words that relate to the story, even if the word is not mentioned in the text. Remind them how you selected the words *prepare*, *preparation*, *team* and *teamwork* for the story of "The Three Little Pigs."

Even though students in the middle grades can read chapter books on their own, it is easier to introduce and practice literature responses with picture books or short stories. This guided lesson is based on *Rudi's Pond* by Eve Bunting.

To build interest and background for the lesson, tell students what you like about the story before you begin reading.

Teacher: I really like this story. Let me describe a few of my favorite scenes. I enjoy the beginning of the story where we hear about all of the things Rudi and the narrator did together. I also like the part where the narrator brings the hummingbird feeder to school. I also found the visits from the hummingbird at school quite poignant.

Have all students ready to listen with pen and paper, then read the book aloud. Invite students to jot down some words or themes they feel are important. When you finish, invite students to share their favorite scene, providing time for four or five students to share.

Teacher: We often think about good stories long after we've completed reading them. Sometimes we think about the characters, other times the problem. Today I'd like to think about something else: theme. Does anyone have an idea of what the theme of a story is?

Students may respond with these kinds of thoughts:

- Theme is something we believe.
- It's stuff that people have known for a long time.
- Theme is a truth.
- Theme is something about how people act anywhere and everywhere.

Teacher: The theme of a story is a truth or a belief—a truth that has been important to people for a long time. It's a statement that is true for anyone, living anywhere, at any time in history. For instance, it could be true for a man living in China in 156 B.C., or a girl living in a space station in 2050, or a child living in St. Louis right now.
Themes are stated in a positive way:

- *Practice makes perfect.*
- *An honorable deed is a reward in itself.*
- *Kindness will be repaid with kindness.*
- *Perseverance pays off.*

At this time, bring out a poster or an overhead of several possible themes like the ones mentioned and have individual children read them aloud for the class.

Teacher: Here are a few examples of what a theme might be. Most good stories have a theme. Different readers often discover different themes for the same story.
To find a theme, let's make a list of some of the important words you jotted down from *Rudi's Pond*.

Place an overhead transparency on the projector and start by listing a few words yourself to spark ideas, such as *friend, sad, poems, memory*.

Next, take words from volunteers until you have a list of 7–10 words. Encourage students to contribute words about how they felt or what the narrator might have been thinking. They will probably offer words like *hummingbird, remember, friendship, heart, not fair, died, sadness, empty* and *missing*.

Teacher: Now, I'm going to start to write some possible themes for this story—something that I believe is true about people that this story shows me. I'm going to use one or two words from our list to begin. (*Write your themes on the overhead projector.*)

Lesson Commentary

The more students are engaged, the more thought that they will bring to their writing.

- *A friend is a treasure.*

- *Friends are there for each other.*

- *You can remember a friend in a lot of ways.*

Teacher: I'm not going to stop yet. I've learned that my best themes usually come after many tries. I'm going to push myself to think more about the story and see what I can come up with.

Continue writing.

- *Friendship is a two-way street.*

- *Friendship is a give and take.*

- *A true friendship lasts forever.*

- *Memories of a lost friend are comforting.*

- *Something made with a friend is a treasure.*

- *A true friend is always in your heart.*

Ask for student volunteers to read your themes aloud. Demonstrate by thinking aloud about how you're going to put a star by the three that seem most important to you.

Teacher: I put a star by these three:

- A friend is a treasure.

- Friends are there for each other.

- A true friendship lasts forever.

I'm going to think about these for a few minutes while you write your own themes. Remember, don't stop after one. Your best themes might appear later in your list. Start with one or two of the words that you listed as important. Think about the story and what happened in it. What truth do you think is shown in the events of this story? Write your themes as positive statements.

Out and About

At this time, I circulate around the room. Not so much to help students who are thinking, but to find things to celebrate in their writing. I make a big deal when I see thoughtful themes written well. Occasionally I'll ask the student writer to share his or her theme with the class. I do this both to reinforce what the writer is doing well and so that others can hear their peers' work and get ideas for their own writing. Sharing with the class does not encourage copying; rather, it spurs student writers to come up with something original of their own.

Allow the students to continue for about ten minutes. If they need more time, give them five more minutes or so, and then ask them to star their three favorites.

Teacher: Now, I'm going back to my list and circling the theme that I feel strongest about—the one that I want to write about in a theme response. I want a theme that can be shown with specific scenes or dialogue from this story. (*Read your three possible themes aloud again.*)

I've decided to select: *Friends are there for each other.* Now I'd like each of you to select the theme from your own list that you feel is the strongest.

After a few moments, ask the students if they would like to share.

The Power of Sharing

❋

To generate even more enthusiasm for this part of the lesson, have 3–4 overhead transparencies available for your students. When they have completed a list of possible themes, invite them to use a marker to write their favorite one on a transparency and to pass the transparencies and markers to other students when they have finished writing.

Share these as a whole group by asking the author of each theme to read his or her contribution. Students of all ages enjoy this activity. One reason is that they enjoy the spontaneous kudos offered by the other students. Another reason is that they often get additional ideas from one another. You can even give a few moments after the sharing if anyone wants to add another theme or two, or revise an existing theme. This process builds confidence in the writer, and it often helps writers fine-tune what they've written. Try it.

After a child reads his or her chosen theme, I like to invite students to comment on anything they feel is noteworthy, even though they have already provided their strongest responses by simply *Ooh*-ing aloud after the reading of a particularly articulate theme. It's fun to watch the writer's reaction to this kind of instantaneous praise.

I usually only allow six or seven students to read their themes before we continue the lesson, but if all of the students are enthusiastic and really want to read, I do take the time. Why squelch this kind of involvement in thinking and literature?

Learning about theme and selecting a theme for a story is plenty of work for one day. This is a natural stopping point in the process. Once students are familiar with theme, these first steps go quickly, and then you might want to proceed into the next phase of writing the theme response.

How Can We Guide Students to Write Their Responses?

If you're picking up the lesson on another day, ask the students to put their themes on their desks. To refresh the story in everyone's mind, ask a student to briefly summarize *Rudi's Pond*, then have the students reread their themes from the day before. It's also advisable to invite 3–4 students to read their themes aloud to build interest and refresh memories.

Teacher: I'm proud that all of you took the time to find a theme for *Rudi's Pond*. Now I'd like to show you a sample theme response so you can see what elements are important for your audience.

Place Theme Response Sample 1 (Overhead 16) for *Rudi's Pond* on the overhead projector and read it aloud twice.

We want to draw students' attention to the different components in a well-written response. If we ask the students to identify these, they are much more likely to include them and write a structured response around their selected themes. If we simply tell or list these components, students are less interested and less committed, and their responses will reflect that. As we analyze the sample, the teacher and students plan a response.

Teacher: Could someone tell me where the author put his theme?

Student: It's up at the top, in the first sentence. *A true friendship lasts forever.*

Teacher: You're right. It is in the first sentence. Could you please come up here and underline the theme in blue for us?

Continue this process by having students identify and find the location of the book's title and the author's name, underlining these in blue, as well.

Teacher: Now, let's look at that lead—three pieces of important information in the first sentence: the title of the book, the author's name, and the writer's choice of theme.

Please take out paper and a pencil, and let's plan our response. I'd like all of you place a large *L* at the top of your paper like this.

Write an *L* in a place that everyone can see.

Beneath the *L*, I'm going to write the theme that I have chosen for the story today.

Go ahead and write the theme you have chosen today beneath your *L*. It may be one of yours, or you may have heard or seen one written by another student that you like. I'll give you a moment.

TRANSPARENCY

L

Theme—Friends are there
for each other.

83

L

Theme—Friends are there
        for each other.

Title—Rudi's Pond

Author—Eve Bunting

Beneath the theme, I'm going to write *Rudi's Pond* so I am sure to include the title for my audience in the literature response. Please do that on your papers, as well.

Under the title, I'm going to write the author's name—*Eve Bunting.* Please add that information to your plan, too.

Now, I'm going to put an *M* on my plan to show what I want to include in the middle of the response. Please, do that on your plans.

Let's go back and reread our sample theme response and see what kinds of information the reader put into his middle. (*Read the middle sentences of sample 1 to the students aloud.*)

What scenes or dialogue did the writer offer to show that a true friendship lasts forever? Can you identify these parts of the story and then underline them on the transparency?

Student: He told how the narrator wrote a poem about Rudi.

Student: He wrote about how Rudi and the narrator played computer games and colored.

Student: He wrote about how the narrator brought the feeder to school.

Student: He wrote about how she saw Rudi sometimes in the window.

Teacher: I can see how the writer found specific examples from the story to show that a true friendship lasts forever. Now, I want to revisit the story and find scenes where the narrator was there for Rudi and Rudi was there for the narrator. I want to find three or four examples to prove that my theme came from this story. (*Think aloud in front of students.*)

I think it's important to show one thing Rudi did for the narrator and the one thing she did for Rudi. I'm going to find some of the stronger examples and decide which ones I want to use.

(*Let students watch as you revisit the book, turning pages and rethinking the story aloud in front of them.*)

1. Rudi came to the narrator's tea parties.
2. When Rudi was ill, the narrator visited him at home, and they would color in bed.
3. They would go on nature hikes together.
4. Rudi helped the narrator paint her garden gate.
5. Together they made a hummingbird feeder.
6. When Rudi was in the hospital, the narrator and her class made a huge get-well card.
7. When Rudi died, the narrator kept the hummingbird feeder with her at school, and then at home to feel close to Rudi.

I don't need all of these examples, so I'm going to choose:

- Rudi and the tea parties
- the narrator visiting Rudi at his home when he's ill
- Rudi painting the garden gate
- the narrator making a huge get-well card

I think I'll use the scenes where she takes the feeder to school and home in my ending. I'll see how it works.

I'm going to add some brief notes to my plan:

M

Rudi—tea parties

nar—visits Rudi when ill

Rudi—painting door

nar—get-well card

Please notice that I did not write complete sentences. This is prewriting—a plan. I only need notes to myself so that I can remember what I want to say in my writing. As you model for the students, make sure to be brief. A brief note is enough to spur a writer to think about the content again. It is not an involved process.

Teacher: I'm going to give each of you time now to think of three or four scenes or parts of dialogue that show your theme—that act like proof of your theme. These need to be taken directly from the story.

It helps if you have multiple copies of the story available so students can take the book to their desks for a few minutes before returning it for another student's use.

I circulate around the room again. This time, my goal is not to stop and do the work for every student, but to praise examples of notes that support his or her choice of theme. Sometimes I do stop and guide a student who is struggling. I do this by asking these kinds of questions:

- *What theme have you chosen?*

- *What happened in the story to make you think of this?*

- *Did something else happen in the story that shows this theme?*

Provide time for 2–4 students to share their plans.

Teacher: Now, I'm ready for an ending thought. Since my theme is *Friends are there for each other*, I want an ending that ties back to that. I said earlier that I thought I wanted to mention how the narrator carried the hummingbird feeder to school, and then home. Let me think how I want to end this.

Remember that a good way to end a literature response is to bring your theme back to yourself in some way. Explain how this theme reflects your own life in some way. (*Think aloud so students can learn from your process.*)

I want to show that in some way Rudi was still there for the narrator, by giving her memories connected to the hummingbird feeder. I also want to show in my writing that the narrator was still there for Rudi because she was holding onto an object that they made together, and choosing not to forget him. I also want

E

hummingbird feeder shows
how they're both still there

my mom's recipes

my dad's red
raspberry bucket

to mention that I have objects like that, too—like my mother's recipes and the bucket my father used for many years to pick his red raspberries.

I think I'm ready to write a note to myself for the ending. First, I'll put an *E* on my plan.

I'd like all of you to stop and reread your theme again. Can you think of one last thought from the story that shows this theme? Has anything ever happened to you that fits this theme? If so, mention that in your ending.

I'll be walking around while you complete your plans.

When most students have written a note for their endings, ask another 2–4 students to share their whole plans.

This is another natural stopping point, especially if this is the first or second time through the process. Students feel a sense of achievement when they have completed their plans. As always, ensure that students keep their plans in a safe place until the next day. And keep in mind that as students write more and more literature responses, the discussion and planning will take less time, and they will be ready to write from their plans immediately.

L

Theme—Friends are there
           for each other.

Title—Rudi's Pond

Author—Eve Bunting

M

Rudi—tea parties

nar—visits Rudi when ill

Rudi—painting door

nar—get-well card

E

hummingbird feeder shows
how they're both still there

my mom's recipes

my dad's red
raspberry bucket

THE LESSON–PART 3

Composing the Theme Response

As I mentioned in the introduction, it's best to keep literature responses short. Your goal is to have children respond frequently with focused thinking. Through brief modeling, you can now show them how to take what's on their plans and write. First, write your lead. Think aloud and remind yourself that you need your chosen theme, the title of the book, and the author's name. You can then point to the lead portion of your plan. Your draft might look something like this:

Eve Bunting, the author of Rudi's Pond, shows us that Friends are there for each other. She develops this theme from the first page, when she explains through the narrator's voice that she and Rudi are friends at school and home.

Ask students:

- *Do I have the author's name?*
- *Did I mention the title of the book?*
- *Is my theme mentioned in this lead?*

Teacher: Now, look at your own plans and craft a one- or two-sentence lead that will pull the reader into your response. Make sure to include all of the information on your plan for the lead, plus an interesting little nugget.

Again, walk around the classroom peeking over shoulders and celebrating any solid or unique leads. When the students have completed their leads, give them a moment to reread and revise, if they like. Ask for volunteers to share their leads. Encourage the class to give positive feedback on what the writers did well. Usually, listening to two or three leads suffices, and the students are ready to move forward.

Continue to use your plan to organize your thoughts for the middle of the response. Write four or five sentences for the middle. It might look something like this:

> Rudi comes to the narrator's home and enjoys tea parties with his friend and her doll. The narrator spends time with Rudi when he's feeling ill. They color and play computer games. One day, they paint tulips on the narrator's garden gate. And when Rudi was in the hospital, the narrator sent a card to him, as well as joined with her classmates to make a big get-well banner.

Ask the students to look at the middle part of their plans and add *specific* details from the story that support the themes they have chosen. Sometimes a student will get an idea that's better than one on his plan, and he will ask if he can substitute. Let that student know that writers often get stronger ideas as they go deeper into the process, and that it is perfectly acceptable to revise as we write.

As the students work, circulate around the room. Point out precise details that add support to a student's theme.

To end the writing portion of the lesson, revisit your plan and read what you have listed for the ending. Model composing a brief ending for students. It might look like this:

> At the end of the story, Eve Bunting has her narrator carry a hummingbird feeder that both friends made back to her house. It is a constant reminder of Rudi, and helps keep his memory alive in her heart. My mother and father were two of my dearest friends. They have both died, but I think of them often. Every time I use one of mom's handwritten recipes it's as if I can hear her voice speaking to me through her handwriting. And one of my dad's greatest loves was his raspberry patch. I still have the old tin bucket that he used to pick his berries. It has a permanent place in my kitchen. So even if a friend is gone, our memories sustain us, and we are once again there for each other.

Launch the students back into writing by asking them to reread their notes for their endings. As they work, walk around the room and mention what they are doing well.

When they pause, ask for a few volunteers to share their endings and receive positive feedback.

*If you feel that
a grade is appropriate,
provide students with
a simple rubric of 3–4
criteria. Read about the
use of rubrics in Chapter
One (page 19). In most
cases, reflecting on and
discussing a response is
the best evaluation a
student can receive.*

Audience

Remember to provide time for students to receive audience feedback, from one another, parents, or even students from another classroom. For ideas on relevant feedback, read the suggestions in the introduction (pages 6–7).

Student Theme Response

❋

Here is a theme literature response written by Kassidy Crowder on the book *Mole Music* by David McPhail.

> If you practice, you can do what you want *like Mole in the book* Mole Music *by David McPhail. I really like this theme, and he practiced, practiced, practiced, and then he could play.*
>
> *After three weeks, Mole could play music. He could also play better than the man on TV. He still practiced, practiced, practiced, and he played beautiful music. Soon he could play some songs that people above ground heard.*
>
> *How do I relate to this theme? Like Mole, I practice the piano. My sister Makayla taught me some notes and I practiced more. Soon I could play a song called "Mary Had a Little Lamb."*

This was Kassidy's first literature response on theme. Following a simple plan and watching as the teacher modeled was all the support she needed to be successful.

To show the variety of student responses, here is another very different response, written by one of Kassidy's classmates, Michala Calhoun.

> *My theme is* Imagination is a good thing. *I think that Mole used his imagination when he played a song in* Mole Music *by David McPhail. His imagination went wild.*
>
> *After a few months, he played beautiful music. When he played bad, the tree died. When he played good the tree above his head grew bigger and bigger. The people that were having a war opened their hearts and imaginations. I like imagination because I like to create things. Once I drew a double-winged horse. Imagination inspires me to get up and create.*

Both of these responses are short, and that's good. They focused on the theme and said what each girl was thinking. Because Kassidy and Michala were successful in a short response, they will be excited about doing more literature responses in the future.

Theme Response

RUBRIC 9

	Excellent	Satisfactory	Needs Work
Structure	Includes lead, middle, and end	Includes two out of the three structural elements	Structure is difficult to identify
Theme and Support	Theme matches story and is supported with four specific examples	Theme is stated and is supported by three examples	Theme is vague and supported by two examples or fewer
Fluency	One thought flows into another throughout the response	Some of the thoughts flow	Response reads like a list

RUBRIC 10

	Excellent	Satisfactory	Needs Work
Lead	Includes title, author, and theme	Includes two of the three lead elements	Includes one or none of the lead elements
Supporting Examples	Response includes at least four examples from the text that support the theme	Response includes three examples from the text that support the theme	Response includes two or fewer examples from the text that support the theme
Focus	All of the writing remains focused on the chosen theme	Some of the writing remains focused on the chosen theme	Little or none of the writing remains focused on the chosen theme

Lesson Review

1. Explain that a theme is a universal truth written as a positive statement.
2. Create purpose for writing by discussing why we want to identify themes.
3. Reread a familiar story to students.
4. List "important" words about the emotional aspects of the story.
5. Write several themes using some of these "important" words.
6. Select the theme that is most relevant.
7. Study an example of a theme literature response and find key components.
8. Create a simple plan for a lead, middle, and end.
9. Compose the literature response, using the plan as a guide.
10. Have students share with an audience and receive feedback on what they did well.

Another Look

Reinforcement Lessons on Theme

Scaredy Squirrel

For this lesson, read the book *Scaredy Squirrel* by Melanie Watt to your class, ideally for the second or third time. Next, brainstorm a list of important words. Your list might contain these:

scared	safe	risk	unknown	happy
advantages	disadvantages	control	predictable	routine
prepared	emergency	plan	panic	incredible
excitement	change	discovery	life	surprise

You and the students can now brainstorm several themes. Some choices might be:

- *Be prepared for the worst, celebrate the best.*
- *Possibilities abound.*
- *The unexpected can be wonderful!*
- *Be open to change.*
- *Living requires a spoonful of risk.*
- *Control creates routine, risk creates adventure.*
- *Adventure is the result of risk.*

- *Be prepared to live.*
- *Be prepared to change.*
- *A little change can be healthy.*

Have students select one theme that seems most relevant. Place Theme Sample 2 (Overhead 17) on the overhead projector and find the key elements. Continue with a brief plan and the writing of the theme response.

Yatandou

For this lesson, read *Yatandou* by Gloria Whelan to your students, ideally for the second or third time. Next, brainstorm a list of important words. It might contain some of these:

sacrifice	work	cooperation	village	pounding
family	play	hope	inspiration	goal
determination	change	improvement	dreams	story

Students can now brainstorm several themes using the words they have listed, including these:

- *Sacrifice multiplies appreciation.*
- *Hope eases sacrifice.*
- *Accomplishing a goal can be its own reward.*
- *Dreams give meaning to work.*
- *Change is necessary to growth.*
- *Cooperation eases the weight of work.*
- *Dreams are attainable.*
- *Story shares the journey.*
- *A moment of play can balance a day of work.*

Have students select the theme that seems most relevant. Place Theme Sample 3 (Overhead 18) on the overhead projector and find the key elements. Continue with a brief plan and the writing of the theme response.

Across the Blue Pacific

Reread *Across the Blue Pacific* by Louise Borden to your students. Then, brainstorm a list of important words from the story and the emotions the story evokes. Your list will probably contains words such as these:

war	friends	hard times	faraway	world
memory	service	brave	safe	message
missing	remember	story	peace	neighbors
ready	important			

Literature Link

Here is a list of other books and stories that lend themselves to a theme response.

How Elephant Got Its Trunk
by Norman Gorbaty

"John Lennon Said"
by Cathy Hopkins
from *Shining On*
by 11 Star Authors
Foreword
by Lois Lowry

The Memory String
by Eve Bunting

"Squealers" in *Part of Me*
by Kimberly Willis Holt

"Trapped" in *Part of Me*
by Kimberly Willis Holt

The White Elephant
by Sid Fleischman

Pink and Say
by Patricia Polacco

You and the students can now brainstorm several themes. Some choices might be:

- *A true friend is never forgotten.*
- *People need to be brave during hard times.*
- *Hard times birth bravery.*
- *A faraway friend is always with us.*
- *Service to others is honorable.*
- *Everyone sacrifices during war.*
- *The world remembers bravery.*
- *Friends create important memories.*
- *Important stories live forever.*

Ask students to select the theme that seems most relevant. Place Theme Sample 4 (Overhead 19) on the overhead projector and find the key elements. Continue with a brief plan and the writing of the theme response.

OVERHEAD 16 ## Rudi's Pond

For me, the theme of *Rudi's Pond* by Eve Bunting is *A true friendship lasts forever*. Rudi and the narrator enjoyed being together. They played computer games, took hikes at a pond, painted a gate and colored. After Rudi died, the narrator still thought of her friend often. She wrote a poem about Rudi. She brought the hummingbird feeder they made to school. When she saw the hummingbird at the window she remembered something Rudi had once said, "If I was a bird, I'd come." As she remembered and missed her friend, she'd sometimes see his face in the window. At the end of the school year, the narrator takes the hummingbird feeder home. It's her way of keeping Rudi with her forever.

I believe that once you have a really good friend, nothing can keep you apart. If your friend moves far away, you can email or write letters and still share what's important with each other. If your friend dies, like Rudi, you have your memories and that friendship is still a part of you—forever.

OVERHEAD 17 ## 2 Scaredy Squirrel

As I read Melanie Watt's book *Scaredy Squirrel*, I kept thinking how *Exploration leads to learning*. I think the author demonstrates this theme by showing us that if we stay in the same old place and do the same old thing, our understanding of the world becomes limited.

Scaredy Squirrel was used to his old nut tree. He knew what to expect, but at the same time, he worried about some things that weren't even a threat to him in his environment, like sharks and Martians. But how would he know that? He never left his tree to really know what was out there. One unfortunate day, Scaredy Squirrel thought he saw a killer bee and he panicked. He accidentally jumped from his tree, only to learn that he was a flying squirrel. In the past, he kept a parachute in his emergency kit, but he learned that he didn't need it. As he glided over the land near his tree, he found out that leaving his tree could be an enjoyable adventure. And even when he finally landed in a bush and stayed there for two hours, he learned that nothing bad necessarily happens outside his tree.

I know that for me, a regular routine feels safe. But when I venture out, like I did last year when I rode the train all by myself to visit my grandparents in Massachusetts, I learn new things. At first I was nervous and worried, but kind people helped me, and it forced me to speak for myself.

Every time I asked a question I learned something new. It's true. Exploration leads to learning.

OVERHEAD 18   **3**   ## Yatandou

Gloria Whelan wrote a picture book about a young girl living in an African Mali village, entitled *Yatandou*. The author introduces us to the theme *Dreams bring hope* when Yatandou describes sleeping on the roof of her home during the hot summer nights. "The sky is my ceiling and the moon my lantern." Her sense of living beyond her immediate world is evident with these words from the beginning of the story.

    Yatandou's dreaming continues throughout the story. She names her weak goat after a famous Mali king, hoping that it, too, will be strong. Her dream for the goat helps her to nurse him into a healthy animal. One day, while Yatandou pounds the millet, she dreams about a new pair of earrings, hoping that her work will bring something of beauty. She also considers what it would be like to go to school and learn from books. Her mind is always planning ahead, dreaming of how life can be better. When Yatandou takes her goat to market, she sells him. Not because she wants to, she cares deeply for her goat. But her mother told her that when they have enough money a machine will come that will chew up the millet and spit out meal. Her dream of having less pounding helps her make the decision to sell her goat and give that money to her mother.

    At the end of the story when she is learning how to write, she signs her pounding stick—the one that used to belong to her mother. She has a new dream—that one day, she will give her pounding stick to her daughter, who will not need it because of her sacrifice and work. This is Yatandou's greatest hope.

OVERHEAD 19   **4**   ## Across the Blue Pacific

As I read the book *Across the Blue Pacific* by Louise Borden, the theme of *The world remembers bravery* seemed to be evident in every scene. Molly Crenshaw recognizes the bravery of her neighbor Ted Walker when his orders take him far away on a submarine in the Pacific Ocean. She realizes that he will be in harm's way and unable to come home anytime soon. She admires his bravery. When Molly studies the huge world map in the hallway at school, she sees the large Pacific Ocean and remembers her friend Ted Walker and how he is on a submarine named The Albacore, cruising those dangerous waters. She knew he was trying to help rescue pilots, take back captured islands and keep an eye on the enemy. Molly appreciated how brave Ted and his fellow crewmates were to go out on patrol for weeks at a time with no mail or telephone calls from loved ones. When Mrs. Walker receives a message that her son Ted is missing in action, Molly sees how her house fills with family and friends who remember Ted and the others who so bravely risked their lives for others. After the war ends, Molly, her family, her neighbors, and others remember Ted Walker and his bravery.